MY TWO LIVES

Jochen "Jack" Wurfl with
Bill Tamulonis and Diane Lonsdale

My Two Lives
All Rights Reserved.
Copyright © 2023 Jochen "Jack" Wurfl with Bill Tamulonis and Diane Lonsdale
www.MyStoryGift.com
410-215-2432

My Story *Gift*

v2.0 r1.0

The opinions expressed in this manuscript are solely the opinions of the author and do not represent the opinions or thoughts of the publisher. The author has represented and warranted full ownership and/or legal right to publish all the materials in this book.

This book may not be reproduced, transmitted, or stored in whole or in part by any means, including graphic, electronic, or mechanical without the express written consent of the publisher except in the case of brief quotations embodied in critical articles and reviews.

Outskirts Press, Inc.
http://www.outskirtspress.com

ISBN: 978-1-4787-3392-8

Cover Photo © 2023 Jochen "Jack" Wurfl with Bill Tamulonis and Diane Lonsdale.
All rights reserved - used with permission.

Outskirts Press and the "OP" logo are trademarks belonging to Outskirts Press, Inc.

PRINTED IN THE UNITED STATES OF AMERICA

To Dana, my daughter, friend, and teammate.
Thank you for inspiring me to tell my story.

TABLE OF CONTENTS

Introduction: My Father's Two Lives i

My First Life
1932-1950

1. Taken 3
2. A Storybook Family 5
3. Scattered 10
4. Hidden 18
5. The Shadow Of Death 29
6. Survival 31
7. Liberation 38
8. Displaced 44

My Second Life
1950 - Present

9. Freedom 53
10. Wings and Roots 59
11. Drafted 68
12. Tour of Duty 73
13. New Beginnings 84
14. Someone Special 91
15. New House, New Babies 96

16. Come Fly with Me	102
17. Diversified	105
18. Pied Piper	112
19. Play Hard	116
20. Off-Balance	132
21. The Loyalty Effect	135
22. Returns	150
23. Love and Patience	159
24. Next Gen	161
25. Ninety and Counting	177

INTRODUCTION: MY FATHER'S TWO LIVES

By Dana Carroll

My father always says that he has lived two lives. He lived his first life in Austria and Germany until age seventeen. From then until now he has lived his second life in America, and says, "Though I've lived here for over 70 years, more things happened to me in my first seventeen."

Jochen ("Jack") Wurfl was born in Dresden, Germany, in 1932, to a Roman Catholic father, Carl, and a Jewish mother, Gretel (nee Baruch). He grew up in Austria, where Carl worked in the office of the president of the country.

Because of his position in the government, my grandfather Carl knew that Adolph Hitler was planning to invade Austria and, in 1937, sent my father and his older brother, my Uncle Peter, to live with their Jewish grandparents in Berlin. To hide their Jewish heritage and stay alive, my father and Uncle Peter were baptized Catholic, joined the Hitler Youth, and saluted *Der Führer* as he paraded down their street every April 20 on his birthday.

Hitler annexed Austria in 1938 (the *Anschluss*) and the new Nazi government sentenced Carl to the Sachsenhausen concentration camp as a political prisoner. Gretel fled to Prague, Czechoslovakia, for safety, but returned to Berlin after Hitler invaded Czechoslovakia.

The next year, when my father turned seven and the Nazi persecution of the Jews intensified, his grandfather sent him and Uncle Peter to hide at a children's summer camp 200 miles away in Dangast, Germany, on the North Sea. They lived there under the protection of a brave, generous woman who they called *Tanta Irma* (Aunt Irma), Irma Franzen-Heinrichsdorff.

In 1941, at nine years old, my father moved back with his mother in Berlin. One day as he and Uncle Peter got off the subway and turned the corner onto their street, they watched as the Gestapo forced their mother into a car and drove her away. They retreated to Tanta Irma's and lived with her until the war ended. Gretel died in Auschwitz, and Carl died of tuberculosis only months after the Americans liberated him.

At age 17, my father came to America as an orphan with Uncle Peter, and the rest is history.

As my sisters and I were growing up, we didn't know much about my dad's childhood. He never talked about it and didn't want to talk about it. But as he got older, he began to revisit his roots and we learned about his life at Tante Irma's, his early years in America, how he met my mother, and how he got into the insurance business.

"Jack, somebody should write a book about your life because it's so amazing," Tom told my father time and time again. But he always answered, "You don't realize it, but there are thousands of lives like mine—people who had a similar childhood, who ended up in another country and found success. Why should I write anything? There's nothing unusual or special about my story."

Tom and I never gave up on the book idea because I felt it was important to document my father's heritage, not just for me, but for the generations of our family and our company team members to come.

Finally, he relented. "I've never been terribly eager to relive my experiences, but you can talk me into anything," he said.

I had never heard some of the stories my father tells in *My Two Lives*. For example, I've seen the pictures of my dad on the beach in Dangast with his parents, looking like they're having a wonderful family time, but never knew that my grandfather had escaped from a concentration camp to get there and was a wanted man.

Many of the stories I had heard before, I had either forgotten or didn't know the context. My dad didn't always tell his stories in chronological order, or talk about what else was going on leading up to the story. Now, with chronology and context, everything he went through makes so much more sense to me.

It is hard to imagine the degree of fear my father lived through with the unimaginable horrors that happened to his parents, grandparents, other family members, and millions of innocent people throughout Europe. The horrific evil that people can inflict on others is impossible to fathom. What my father and Uncle Peter did to survive, and the number of close calls when they might not have made it out of Germany alive, is really unbelievable. One day when I read parts of the manuscript out loud to my husband Tom, I teared up, and couldn't speak at certain points.

Now, we have this treasure of memories that will outlive everybody who reads them today. Thank you, Dad, for telling your story. It is truly God's blessing to have you and to preserve your legacy for the generations.

MY FIRST LIFE
1932-1950

You are my hiding place;
You preserve me from trouble;
You surround me with songs of deliverance.
Psalm 32:7

Chapter 1

Taken

BERLIN, GERMANY, 1942

"HERE, TAKE THIS envelope," my mother told my brother Peter and me, and gave us directions to the delivery location. "When you come up from the subway station, a man will meet you there and give you his code name. Give him the envelope, and he'll give you one to bring back to me."

I was nine years old, and Peter was almost eleven. We guessed that the envelopes contained messages to and from my father, who was a prisoner in a German concentration camp but still communicated with my mother and the Resistance through the Gestapo guards he bribed.

Peter and I exchanged envelopes with the man and rode the subway back home. As we walked away from the subway station and turned the corner onto Meineke Street, we saw Gestapo and SS cars up the road in front of our apartment and stopped in our tracks. We decided to wait for the cars to leave, then go home and ask our mother what the police were doing there. But then we watched the agents take her out of our apartment, force her into a car, and drive her away.

We had overheard our parents and grandparents talking about their friends and relatives who had disappeared, but why are they taking our mother? Where are they taking her?

Peter and I looked at the envelope, then at each other. We didn't dare open it but figured whatever was inside would get us, our parents, the man who gave it to us, and anyone else whose name appeared in it into big trouble. We ran back down into the subway station, ripped the envelope to shreds, and threw it in a trash can.

We couldn't get into our apartment because the Gestapo sealed the front door with a sign displaying a swastika and the warning: RESTRICTED AREA. NO TRESPASSING. CIVILIANS WILL BE EXECUTED. Now what?

Peter called the person my mother gave us as an emergency contact in case this ever happened—her lawyer, Alwin Grossman—who found a place for us to stay. Then we set out on a mission to find our mother. I don't remember how, but a couple of days later we found out that the Nazis were holding her at the Alt-Moabit prison in downtown Berlin. *We'll take our chances with the Nazis. We've got to go see her!*

We took the subway downtown and walked into the prison. It's a miracle that we got inside—I guess the guards didn't pay much attention to young kids. We walked up a couple of levels and in one of the long corridors, stopped to look out the window. A group of prisoners meandered around below in a courtyard—it must have been exercise time.

There's Mom!

We watched and waited until my mother went back inside, then searched from floor to floor to find her. Guards were all over the place, but we ignored them and they ignored us.

There she is!

We rushed to her cell. "Mom, what's happening?"

She didn't take the time to explain. She said that she loved us and told us to study hard in school, then ordered us to leave because she was afraid we would end up in the prison with her. As we walked away from our mother's cell, guards spotted us and figured out that we had come to see a prisoner. They grabbed us but we wrestled away from them and took off running as fast as we could. The guards chased us but couldn't catch us and gave up once we escaped out the prison gate onto the streets.

I never saw my mother again. Peter and I fled by train back to our hiding place 200 miles away in Dangast, Germany, on the North Sea, and the Nazis sentenced my mother to Auschwitz.

Chapter 2

A Storybook Family

Think of all the beauty in yourself and in everything around you and be happy.
- Anne Frank, *The Diary of a Young Girl*

GUTENSTEIN, AUSTRIA, 1932-1936

INTERFAITH MARRIAGES WERE rare in the 1920s and 1930s, and so taboo that when my Roman Catholic father, Karl Wurfl, married my Jewish mother, Margaret, he was excommunicated from the Church.

Divorce was also rare, but both of my parents were previously married and divorced. Maybe they got together after their divorces, or maybe their getting together is why they divorced their previous spouses, I don't know. I'm just glad my parents didn't listen to people who told them what they couldn't do.

In the year I was born, 1932, most European women delivered their babies at home with the help of a midwife. As the time of my birth approached, my mother, who everyone called Gretel, traveled over 300 miles by train to her parents' home in Dresden, Germany. There my grandmother could provide additional help with the new grandchild.

I was born on June 15. My parents never told me how or why they chose the name Jochen, and I never asked. There were no Jochens on the family tree so as far as I can tell, they picked it out of thin air.

Soon after my birth, my mother took me home to my father and my seventeen-month-old brother, Peter, in Gutenstein, Austria, a small village with a population of about 1,800 located 40 miles northeast of Vienna.

FAMILY TREES

My mother came from a German family, the Cohns, who reached millionaire status from their popular department store on Wilhelm Street in Bernburg and their other real estate holdings in Germany. My grandmother, Lina Cohn, married Ferdinand Baruch, a World War I veteran of the German Army and recipient of the Iron Cross for combat heroism. Ferdinand joined my grandmother's brothers, Willy and Adolf, in the Cohn family business as a partner.

My grandparents, Ferdinand and Lina Baruch

My grandparents lived an affluent lifestyle in their early years. They moved from Dresden to the capital city, Berlin, and socialized with business owners, professors, and others in the higher social strata. They collected art—including a model of the Stephan Sinding sculpture, Valkyrie, that's now on display at a museum in Denmark, and three paintings by Lovis Corinth, whose works have sold for over $1 million. And they spoiled their only child, Gretel, my mother.

I know very little about my father's family other than they were a Catholic family from Linz, Austria. My father had four brothers, and two sisters who both became Catholic nuns. I don't know much about my father as a young man either, other than he served in the Austrian Navy and was stationed on battleships on the Mediterranean Sea. I know that only because I found postcards he sent to his parents updating them about the ships he was on.

My father had one son, also named Karl, from his first marriage. Karli, as I called him, was about eight years older than me. Peter and I always looked forward to his visits because he taught us how to play soccer and other "big boy" games.

HOLLYWOOD MATERIAL

I can still picture our two-story home in Gutenstein, with the hedge where the porcupines grazed. Mountains surrounded us, and on Sundays we hiked the paths and trails. One particular steep, rocky trail leading into the mountains was always crawling with huge snails, but they never deterred us because we had a bigger purpose: lunch at the top of Artz mountain at a restaurant owned by a friend of my father's.

Not that we ate out often because my mom was a great cook. Like most women in that era, she graduated from "home economics" school where they taught cooking, housekeeping, and child-rearing.

Besides hiking, winter sports were popular in Austria. My father, six feet tall and athletic, was an avid skier and bobsledder. Peter and I loved to frolic in the snow.

My father worked for the office of the chancellor of Austria, Kurt von Schuschnigg, and was stationed in Vienna. He commuted by train, and Peter and I loved meeting our dad when he got off the train, mostly because we were happy to see him, and partly because we were mesmerized when the train circled the turntable and headed back north.

Winter sports were popular in Austria. I'm on the sled between my mother and Peter while my father skis

Growing up in Austria, the home of Mozart, classical music is all we heard in the house. I've always liked Mozart, and Haydn—all light, pleasant music. I also enjoy Wagner, and Strauss's Vienna music. Vienna is the birthplace of the waltz, and my mother took Peter and me to dance lessons. "Everybody in Austria waltzes," she said.

My mother's only worry was the Roma nomads—Gypsies. She didn't like us playing in the front yard because it was common for Gypsies to ride down the street in their horse-drawn wagons and steal children. Always the protective mother, whenever she heard a wagon coming down the street she'd run outside and hold onto Peter and me.

Gypsies excepted, our family was living such a storybook life in our early

A STORYBOOK FAMILY

I'm on the left in this still image taken from the home movies Hedy Lamarr shot for our family

years in Gutenstein that my father asked Austrian-born Hollywood movie star Hedy Lamarr, who was a good friend of both of my parents, to bring her film crew to our house and shoot home movies of our family. I'm so lucky to still have the footage. I only wish she had popped herself into one of the scenes.

THE STORY TURNS

I don't know how my father knew Hedy Lamarr, but he might have dated her after divorcing his first wife. I've lost it but I once had a clipping from a Vienna newspaper that mentioned the two of them driving together in my father's car, so they had some kind of friendship. The story made the news because my father accidentally ran into a policeman.

Most people remember Hedy Lamarr only as a steamy actress, but she played integral roles in the Allied victory in World War II, and the development of the cell phone.

Soon after Adolf Hitler was appointed Chancellor of Germany in 1933, Hedy Lamarr's first husband, a Jewish weapons manufacturer named Fritz Mandl, began building tanks for Hitler's war machine.

Hitler rose to power on his Nazi party's promise to restore Germany's pride and stature on the world stage after its defeat in World War I. He planned to replace Germany's democracy with a dictatorship, rid Europe of Jews and other non-Aryan ethnic groups, and lead Germany on a campaign for world conquest.

Hedy Lamarr accompanied her husband to numerous dinners and other affairs with Hitler and his ally, Italian dictator Benito Mussolini. She was also Jewish and was so appalled by what she heard about their military operations that she fled to Austria and shared her first-hand knowledge with Austrian and other European governments.

She was also an inventor who designed wings for Howard Hughes's airplanes, a torpedo guidance system used by the U.S. Navy, and the technology that formed the basis of WiFi, GPS, and Bluetooth communication systems.

Because of his position in the Austrian government, my father knew that Hitler had set his nationalistic and expansionist sights on the *Anschluss*—the reunification of Germany with Austria, Hitler's birthplace, and once part of the German empire. When Austrian Chancellor Schuschnigg put my father in charge of distributing instructions to Austrian citizens on how to wear gas masks, my father feared for our family.

"We have to at least get the boys out of here," he told my mother, "to someplace they will be invisible and safe." In 1936, our storybook life turned to a more ominous chapter.

Chapter 3

SCATTERED

We'll leave of our own accord and not wait to be hauled away. Don't you worry. We'll take care of everything. Just enjoy your carefree life while you can.

-Otto Frank, to his daughter Anne

BERLIN, GERMANY, 1936-1939

MY MOTHER'S PARENTS, Ferdinand and Lina Baruch, lived in a huge apartment on Schlüter Street in Berlin. They were both Jewish, but in 1936 Berlin was a cosmopolitan city where people with diverse religious and political beliefs still coexisted peacefully, even with the Nazis, so my parents took Peter and me to Berlin to live with my grandparents.

For a four-year-old who had just arrived in Berlin and lived with his wealthy grandparents, life was good.

Every Sunday my grandfather, Peter, and I walked eight blocks from our apartment to the Zoologischer Garten Berlin, the 86-acre zoo with its 12,000 birds, crocodiles,

Every Sunday my grandfather took Peter and me to the Berlin Zoo
Photo credit: Paul Sableman, Wikimedia Commons

snakes, hippopotamuses, giraffes, sharks, lions, tigers, and bears—over 2,000 species in total. Money was no object for my grandfather. He paid around 5,000 Reichsmarks for shares of stock in the zoo, which, in place of dividends, gave shareholders free access to the zoo.

On the way, we always stopped for ice cream at the outdoor café at the Hotel Kempinski, and before going home we would play for a while in the amusement park, which, alongside the zoo, comprised the 520-acre *Großer Tiergarten* (Great Zoo).

All grandparents love to show off their grandchildren, and mine enjoyed watching Peter and me waltz so much that every time they invited friends for dinner, which was several times a week, they would call us in and say, "Dance for our company." We would assume the proper dance positions—Peter always took the lead—and waltz around the room. We were embarrassed, but we wanted to please our grandparents.

After our performance, all the men would retire to my grandfather's *Herrenzimmer* (men's room)—the room with the big cushy chairs that no one else was allowed to go near—to smoke cigars and talk business and politics.

We lived around the corner from the *Kurfürstendamm*, a wide boulevard lined with fancy stores and restaurants. One day while we were there I saw a crowd in front of a store window staring at a box with black and white pictures flashing all around. "That's a television," someone said. "Someday we're all going to have a television." My grandparents collected a lot of art but never owned a television.

Life was good but I had a scary bout with scarlet fever. I spent several weeks in isolation in the hospital, and when my mother came to visit she could only look at me from the other side of a glass window. When the doctors released me from the hospital they would not let me go anywhere around other children, not even my brother. I lived with an uncle for a month or two before moving back with my grandparents and Peter.

NOT A NORMAL WAY OF LIFE

Our life was calm and stable, but in the 1930s, Jews in Berlin were not entitled to a completely normal way of life. Jews were not considered German citizens and were forbidden to fly the German flag. It was against the law for Jews to

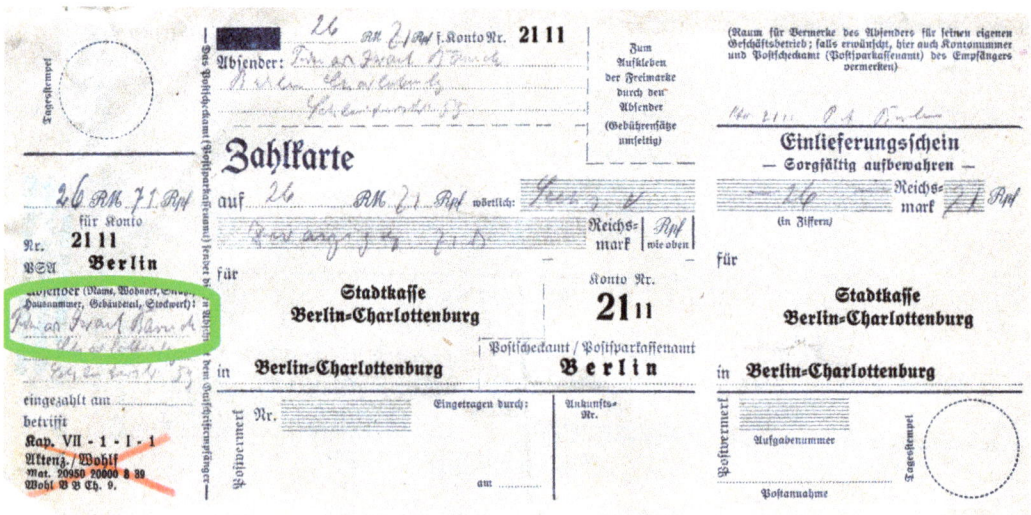

My grandfather's signature (green circle) appears on this police citation issued to my grandmother for attempting to buy coffee beans, a delicacy forbidden to Jews

marry Germans. Jews were barred from holding civil service and university positions, and Jewish doctors were not allowed to practice in German hospitals.

Jews could not go to the grocery store and buy the same groceries as gentiles. One day my grandmother asked to buy coffee beans. The storekeeper reported her to the police and they slapped her with a fine of 25 Reichsmarks. Only imitation coffee made from acorns, chicory, or some other roasted grain for the Jews.

Students burned books written by Jews and about Jews at public bonfires under the orders of Joseph Goebbels, the Minister of Propaganda and Public Enlightenment. *Time* Magazine described one of the book-burning rallies:

> "Undampened by a chilly drizzle, some 40,000 Germans jammed the square between Berlin's Friedrich Wilhelm University and the Opera House.
>
> Toward midnight a procession entered the square, headed by officers of the University's student dueling corps in their dress uniforms. Behind them came other students and a line of motor trucks piled high with books. More students clung to the trucks, waving flaring torches that they hurled through the air at the log pile. Blue flames of gasoline shot up, the

Books burning in Berlin
Photo credit: Wikimedia Commons

pyre blazed. One squad of students formed a chain from the pyre to the trucks. Then came the books, passed from hand to hand.

While the flames flared highest, up to a little flag draped rostrum stumped club-footed, wild-eyed little Dr. Paul Joseph Goebbels, Minister of Propaganda and Public Enlightenment in the Nazi Cabinet, organizer of the great midnight bibliocaust. (22 May 1933)

Peter and I were never allowed outside late at night so we never witnessed a book burning, but we heard about them, and we listened to Joseph Goebbels's propaganda speeches every week in school.

Because of the discrimination against Jews, my parents took Peter and me to a Catholic church to be baptized when we arrived in Berlin. That way, whenever the Nazis asked for our identification papers, they would see "Catholic" as our religion.

My grandparents celebrated the major Jewish holidays at home but did not attend synagogue, and they did not raise Peter and me as either Jewish or Catholic in any way. Under the Nazis, it wasn't a good idea to outwardly practice any kind of religion because Nazis could not tolerate any autonomous institution that might compete for someone's allegiance to the Reich.

HEIL HITLER

Week by week and month by month, Hitler became more and more visible. I don't remember much about the 1936 Summer Olympic games in Berlin, but I remember the commotion throughout the city and all the pictures and movie clips of Hitler at the *Reichssportfeld* (Imperial Sports Field). He didn't look happy whenever an American or black athlete won a gold medal—American track star Jesse Owens won four—and wouldn't shake their hands as he did with all the other winners.

Every April 20th, Hitler celebrated his birthday by parading down the *Kurfürstendamm*. We lived right around the corner and ran out to the curb to catch a glimpse of him as he rode by. The street bulged with onlookers but Peter and I wormed our way to the front to get a good look at him standing up in his car and waving to the cheering crowds. Some cheered because they believed in Nazism, while others, including Peter and me, were putting on an act to protect themselves and their families from persecution, imprisonment, or worse.

As Hitler's visibility and control of the government increased, he tightened his grip on the German population, including Berliners, and life grew more dangerous.

The Nazis introduced military training to boys at a young age. In first grade, my class was not allowed to go home and play after school. We had to stay after and line up outside to practice marching formations and the "Heil Hitler" salute.*

At age six, almost every non-Jewish boy in Berlin—including my Catholic brother and me—joined *Hitlerjugend* (Hitler Youth), which Hitler set up to indoctrinate young boys in Nazi beliefs. Parents who refused to enroll their sons lost their jobs or were imprisoned. Boys who didn't belong were often attacked and beaten by Hitler Youth gangs.

Hitler modeled his new youth group after the Boy Scouts, which he had disbanded. I had fun wearing my uniform (shorts, shirt, and tie) to the weekly meetings, marching, and hiking.

Physical fitness and sports made it fun also. We trained and played every week, and competed in the annual Hitler Youth Olympics against other kids in our local area. And what young boy wouldn't love throwing hand grenades and shooting real rifles and a *Panzerfaust?* (bazooka)? They painted tanks on the side of the school building wall for target practice.

The part of Hitler Youth that bothered Peter and me was the songs they made us sing. Some vilified and threatened Jews:

> *We are standing on the North Sea*
> *Steel-worthy fighters*
> *Ready to fight*
> *The danger of the Jews*

Other songs praised and exalted the Third Reich:

> *We will continue the march,*
> *Even if everything shatters;*
> *Freedom rose in Germany,*
> *And tomorrow the world belongs to it.*

The songs made me wonder what people have against the Jews, but I never came up with a good answer. Peter and I sometimes asked each other, "What are we doing in the Hitler Youth?" We always arrived at the same answer: We have to go along and sing the songs so we won't be found out. We wanted to stay alive.

ENEMY OF THE STATE

Back home in Austria, my father's worst fears became reality on March 11, 1938, when Hitler demanded that Austrian Chancellor Schuschnigg surrender all power to the Nazis or face an invasion. After France and Britain declined to support Austria, Schuschnigg resigned. The next day, German troops crossed the border into Austria, and even Hitler was surprised when thousands of Austrians lined the streets to cheer their arrival.

On March 15, Hitler arrived in Vienna amidst more cheering crowds, but my father was not among them. The Nazis arrested my father and Schuschnigg, charged them as "incorrigible enemies of the state" and shipped them away together on the same train to the Sachsenhausen concentration camp outside of Berlin.

My father's four brothers didn't take any chances on the Nazis coming after them—they took off for Spain. But they were nearly killed in the crossfire of the Spanish Civil War so they migrated to Cuba and eventually settled in Quito, Ecuador. Some of my Jewish cousins on my mother's side of the family fled to Palestine to live in what later became the nation of Israel.

OUR HIDING PLACE

In Berlin, the Nazis dialed up their persecution of the Jews in hopes they would leave the country. The Nazis forced Jews to register their property—a prelude to confiscating it all.

The zoo forced my grandfather and all Jewish shareholders to sell their stock at a loss, and the Nazis turned the zoo's concert halls and auditoriums into showplaces for their propaganda.

My grandfather worried about the future of Jews in Berlin and feared that Peter and I were no longer invisible or safe. A lawyer friend told him about *"Irmenfried"* (Irma Peace), a children's summer camp in the resort village of Dangast, 200 miles northwest of Berlin on the North Sea, operated by a woman named Irma Franzen-Heinrichsdorff.

Our house and gardens at Irmenfried

In 1938, My grandfather arranged for Peter and me to hide away at Irmenfried temporarily. But "temporarily" turned into twelve years, and *"Tante Irma"* (Aunt Irma), as I called her, saved our lives and became our second mother.

*Author's Note:

I stumbled across my first-grade picture which appeared in *Time* Magazine purely by accident.

In the year 2000, my daughter Lisa was shopping at the Hutzler's department store for my Christmas present and spotted *Great Images of the 20th Century* in the book section. *Hmmm. It's a new millennium, Dad always talks about history… yeah!*

How sweet of her, and what a nice book!

I didn't pick the book up until after New Year's. One night before going to bed I started flipping through the pictures…President Roosevelt, Muhammad Ali, Marilyn Monroe, Neil Armstrong, Vietnam.

I turned to page 31. *Oh, my god! This is my first-grade class! And this is me! The two boys next to me were my best friends!*

The picture was taken in the back of my school in Berlin while we were practicing the Hitler salute, and 68 years later, my daughter buys a book for her dad for Christmas and there's a picture of me in it! What are the chances of that? To see me and my classmates and the school, and to show the picture to my family and friends was the strangest feeling in the world.

Chapter 4

HIDDEN

I have often been downcast but never in despair; I regard our hiding as a dangerous adventure, romantic and interesting at the same time.

- Anne Frank, *The Diary of a Young Girl*

DANGAST, GERMANY, 1938-1942

TANTE IRMA PUT Indian feathers in her hair, and the game was on! We emerged from our tepees—the Apaches from Irmenfried, with our faces painted and headdresses fixed—and set out to rescue our princess from the Cherokees, our classmates from Dangast, who kidnapped her.

Playing Indians at Tante Irma's

Inspired by the German author Karl May's books about American Indians, Indian games were one of our favorite pastimes at Tante Irma's children's camp, our hiding place.

During the summer months, 30 children from all over Germany joined the fun at the camp. Our day began with jumping jacks, pushups, toe touches, and other calisthenics led by either Tante Irma or her daughter, Waltraud, who was seventeen when I first arrived.

After breakfast, we'd either stay around the campground and play Indians or hit the beach on the North Sea. At the beach, we'd swim when the tide was in and play in the *Schlick* (silt) when the tide went out. At low tide, the water in the North Sea receded fifteen feet or more and we'd run out and slosh around in the mud. It took a while to clean ourselves up afterward but the minerals were healthy for our skin—so healthy that tourists came to Dangast for mud baths.

On rainy days Tante Irma and Waltraud organized indoor games and crafts. They were experts in fun.

When summer camp ended, it left Peter and me, ages seven and six, with Tante Irma, Waltraud and her brother, Gernot, who was four years younger than her, and an Estonian girl around my age named Eva Marita Wiedermann Schmutz. Eva had lived in Berlin with her mother but her mother sent her to Irmenfried. Eva's family was not Jewish, so I'm not sure why she came.

Tante Irma (center) with her daughter, Waltraud, and son, Gernot
Photo credit: "From Dangast to Colorado Springs," by Gert Groning

It wasn't long before Tante Irma welcomed a fourth foster child to Irmenfried. Hans Kaal, who asked us to call him Kotja, was a boy my age from Estonia. Kotja's father, who was a judge in Estonia, brought Kotja to Irmenfried in part to escape the Russian threat to Estonia, and in part because the climate in Dangast was better for Kotja's chronic bronchitis. As we grew up together, Kotja became like a half-brother to Peter and me.

Tante Irma treated all of us like her own children. On our birthdays she let us choose what we wanted for our birthday dinner. I always picked bean soup and I'd eat at least six bowls.

She made Christmas special for us also. Three days before Christmas Eve she would lock the dining room door, declare it off-limits to us kids, and turn it into the "Christmas Room." On Christmas Eve she'd let us in and we'd find it decorated to the hilt, cookie and candy trays everywhere, and a big, beautiful tree with flaming wax candles hanging on the branches (fire hazard? what fire hazard?) and toys or ice skates for each of us wrapped underneath. Everything in the Christmas Room was hard to come by with the shortages and strict rationing limits, but Tante Irma was a clever woman and always managed to have something for us.

Germany's First Female Landscape Architect

Education was a top priority for Tante Irma. She sent Peter and me to the village school in Dangast, about a mile walk each way. Twenty children filled a two-room schoolhouse—first to fourth grades in one classroom, fifth through eighth in the other.

The first time Peter and I walked into the school bathroom we thought, *Uh-oh.* It had one long urinal trough where the boys stood side-by-side. Would our classmates recognize a circumcision if they saw one? Would they realize what

Education was a priority for Tante Irma. Here, Waltraud helps me (head down), Peter (to my left) and two classmates with our homework

it meant? We couldn't take a chance. From then on we waited until all the other boys were finished before we used the bathroom, and if someone came in after us, we'd turn sideways as far as we could.

Our teacher, a close friend of Tante Irma's named Edo Pille, lived above the classrooms with his wife and three sons. I became best friends with *Herr Pille's* (Mr. Pille's) youngest son, Heiko.

Our schoolhouse in Dangast

I loved math—it's so logical! Calculators didn't exist so I learned to compute in my brain. In later work life, I sat around tables with people using calculators and I usually beat them to the answer. Waltraud often helped me with my homework, and I adored her. "I'm going to marry you someday," I always told her. "Ok, my little man," she would say.

Tante Irma taught us horticulture. She gave each of us a 20-square-foot garden plot and showed us how to grow plants and vegetables. Tante Irma was a master gardener and holds the distinction of being Germany's first woman university graduate in landscape architecture. No wonder her greenhouse and garden with acres of lush, exotic plants and trees took visitors' breath away.

Tante Irma told me that her parents didn't want her to go to college. "Women just don't do that," they said. But that didn't stop her. "I can and I will," she said.

After earning her degree she asked her father for a portion of her inheritance to finance the construction of a plant nursery. But her father threatened to disinherit her altogether if she pursued any professional aspirations in horticulture, and offered instead to purchase the children's summer camp in Dangast for her to operate. As a divorced mother with two children and no other source of funds, she had no choice but to accept his ultimatum.

Now, here she was a few years later, risking her life and her children's lives

My shrimp boat on the North Sea

A good catch on the shrimp boat! I'm on the left.

by hiding two half-Jewish boys in her home.

School started at 8 am and ended at 1 pm. After a quick lunch, I went to work either on one of the large farms in Dangast or out on a shrimping boat on the North Sea. If we didn't work, we didn't eat because all the husbands, fathers, and older brothers who would ordinarily be fishing and plowing had been drafted into the German Army.

On the farm, we grew our main staple—potatoes—plus radishes, beans, and other vegetables. There was a shortage of sugar in Germany so we grew sugar beets and extracted the sugar from the roots. We also tended to Tante Irma's prized apple tree on which she grafted four varieties of apples into one juicy new breed. But my favorite job on the farm was driving a team of horses to cut rye and wheat and dig up potatoes in the fields. Every young boy loves to drive something, and how cool to plow by jockeying horses!

I enjoyed working on the shrimp boats more than on the farm because I loved the beautiful North Sea with its strong tides, and I came ashore every day with dinner.

The shrimp boats were big enough only for Captain Blanke and two mates—two kids—and ran on an old diesel engine. "Someday, I'm going to have a boat like this, and I'm going to be the captain," I told myself.

The tides dictated our fishing schedule. We'd go out with the tide and fish until the tide came back in. Sometimes the tide didn't go out until 1 am so we'd fish through the night and get back the next afternoon. That meant I'd miss school so I took my books with me on the boat to keep up with the lessons.

We caught shrimp with two big nets, one on each side of the boat. We'd cast the nets, wait about an hour, then pull them in with a *Winde* (winch, pulley) powered by the boat's engine and hope for a good catch. We'd sort the shrimp by size and steam them in a big pot over a fire right on the boat because we had no refrigeration and the shrimp would have spoiled by the time we reached land.

We always caught other fish in the nets along with the shrimp. One of my favorite foods was—and still is—smoked eel. The most delicious food. They look like snakes but, oh my, once I tried eel a few times, I couldn't live without it.

We ate our fill on the way back to shore, sold steamed shrimp and fish to customers waiting for us at the docks, and took the rest home for the family.

The World at War

Tante Irma kept in touch with my grandfather, who sent her money every month for our support, and with my mother, who faced increased persecution by the Nazis. The violence against the Jews reached new heights in November 1938, just after my grandfather sent Peter and me to Irmenfried. On *Kristallnacht* (Night of Broken Glass) mobs vandalized Jewish-owned businesses, synagogues, and homes, leaving a sea of broken glass on the streets. Even worse, on that one night, the *Schutzstaffel* (Protection Squadrons, aka SS) arrested 30,000 Jewish men and hauled them away to concentration camps.

A Jew and the wife of a political prisoner, my mother fled to Prague, Czechoslovakia to escape the now life-threatening danger in Berlin. In August of 1939, she wrote to Tante Irma and thanked her for protecting her sons:

My Dear Lady,
   Much heartfelt thanks for your endearing letter for my birthday, which made me especially happy as well as giving much happiness.

You're bringing much understanding to our present situation, which makes me thankful and happy to know that my boys are being guarded and taken care of by you.

I tell you honestly and openly that I have many doubts whether it is correct to leave the boys an entire year in the country and to let them attend the village school. But then I say to myself, it is much more important to know that my boys are in an atmosphere in which they will continue to grow and they will be kept alive.

The feelings that I have for you, Dear Lady, that I know that you will continue to raise them so that they will know and respect their parents and they will continue to love their parents and not forget them in spite of this long separation. But above all, it gives me the feeling and understanding which comes above any other concerns and gives me the strength to cope with the fate that has been forced upon me and to live with patience and the belief and the hope that my boys will not slip away from me. I think that this egotism that I am entitled to, meaning that my boys will be saved. Both of my boys are bright and they will know how to catch up in any area, such as writing, mathematics, and languages. All of this one can later learn and catch up, but the feelings are a different story. It is because of that, dear one, that you make me especially happy that my boys are with you as I have the overwhelming feeling that as long as the boys are in your care, they will not become strangers to their parents.

It is not now the time to talk about Christmas presents, but I am anxious to clear up a misunderstanding of which I have become aware of since receiving your letter. I want you to know that my husband gave Dr. Wienholtz's attorney last January 50 marks with precise instructions to immediately send you this money. This money was for Christmas presents. Something my husband brought that money in addition to the other money for the children and I will now ask for a confirmation that this money was sent to you. We certainly expect them to follow my husband's instructions. In any case, the money was deposited with instructions to be sent to you.

If you again have a little bit of time, I would again be so happy to receive a few lines from you. To you with much love and health, I

This is my mother's original handwritten letter to Tante Irma:

HIDDEN

remain yours with many greetings for you and kisses for the boys.
Gretel Wurfl

The world became more dangerous for everyone on September 1, 1939, the day that nearly 1.5 million German troops invaded Poland, the attack that prompted England and France to declare war on Germany and triggered World War II. Poland surrendered in less than a month, and weeks later, the SS rounded up Polish Jews into enclosed districts—squalid ghettos where most died from starvation, disease, or execution. Those who survived the ghettos were deported to concentration camps and forced into hard labor.

I had an idea of the horrors going on because, on evenings when Tante Irma wasn't around, Peter and I would tune in to the *verboten* (forbidden) BBC broadcasts out of England on her radio. And every day, after school ended, we'd see Herr Pille hop on his motorcycle dressed in his black SS uniform and ride away.

Yes, my teacher was a Nazi SS officer.

I didn't know what Herr Pille ever did in the SS, but I knew for sure that he was a teacher first and an SS agent second, and he wouldn't have done anything to hurt Tante Irma.

He knew that Peter and I were half-Jewish and that Tante Irma was hiding us, but he never reported us to anyone else, though he had plenty of opportunities. Every once in a while Herr Vogel, the Gestapo officer stationed in Dangast in charge of rounding up Jews and enemies of the Reich, made rounds through the village homes and asked about the people living in them. He came to Tante Irma's several times and asked her, "Who are these boys? Where did they come from?"

I loved my teacher, Herr Pille

They're my adopted boys and they're living here with me," she would say. I'm sure Herr Vogel also asked Herr Pille about us since he lived in Dangast and taught us. Herr Pille knew that we weren't legally adopted but never contradicted Tante Irma's story. He cared enough about us to risk getting shot if someone found out he was protecting us.

I was never afraid of Herr Pille, even when he made our class sing the Hitler Youth songs that disparaged the Jews. To me, he was a nice man and a dedicated teacher. I loved him.

Family Reunions

One day Peter and I were playing at the beach, right below the brick dike. We looked up. We gasped, and our eyes popped wide as saucers.

Mom and Dad! How can this be?

We ran and leaped into their arms.

Growing up I never knew my father to be a Houdini but twice in our first few years at Tante Irma's, desperate to see his family, he escaped from the Sachsenhausen concentration camp, rendezvoused with my mother, and the two of them visited Peter and me.

They played Indians with us and took us to the beach. Once I took them out on the shrimp boat for the day. But after a few days with us, villagers would start asking them too many questions—"What are you doing here? Why aren't you fighting in the German Army?"—and they would disappear without saying goodbye.

My father escaped from his concentration camp twice to visit us at Irmenfried. Left to right: Kotja, me, Dad, Peter, and Eva.

The SS would eventually catch up to my father and punish him. After his first escape, the prison commander assigned him to *Stiefelgeher* (boot walker) duty. Boot walkers tested boots to help the army determine the best kind of leather for combat boots, but really it was torture. If the boot walker wore a size twelve, they would make him squeeze into a size seven, strap a bag of rocks on his back, and force him to walk around a quarter-mile circle until he collapsed.

Most boot walkers dropped dead after a few weeks, but my father somehow survived and escaped to visit us with Mom a second time.

Between 1939 and 1941, Germany invaded Denmark, Norway, the Netherlands, Belgium, Luxembourg, France, Yugoslavia, Greece, and the Soviet Union. They massacred 34,000 Jews near Kyiv, Ukraine, and opened a concentration camp at Auschwitz. They also invaded Czechoslovakia, where my mother had fled to its capital city, Prague, for safety.

Trapped in German-occupied Prague by the occupied countries surrounding her, my mother must have thought that if everyone in our family had to live in fear of the Nazis, we should live together. In 1941, she returned to Berlin where my father was in prison and my grandparents still lived. She asked Tante Irma to put Peter and me on a train to Berlin to live with her in an apartment on Meineke Street.

Chapter 5

THE SHADOW OF DEATH

Night after night, green and gray military vehicles cruise the streets. They knock on every door, asking whether any Jews live there... No one is spared. The sick, the elderly, children, babies, and pregnant women—all are marched to their death.

-Anne Frank, *The Diary of a Young Girl*

BERLIN 1941-1942

"YOUR MOTHER IS back in Berlin and she wants you to stay with her," Tante Irma told Peter and me.

I enjoyed living at Tante Irma's but was thrilled to be with my mother. I started school and made new friends, but Berlin was scarier than when I left only a couple of years before. When I first returned I noticed that some people walking on the streets wore a big yellow Star of David on their chests, and some didn't. When someone wearing the star saw someone without a star walking toward them, they would step off the sidewalk into the street to let the person without the star pass by.

Inscribed in the middle of the star was the word *Jude* (Jew). Nazi minister of propaganda Joseph Goebbels instituted the star, which he called a "general distinguishing mark" for Jews as a way to stigmatize them and, ultimately, segregate them and facilitate their deportation to concentration camps. My mother wore a star—the "Jewish badge" as the Nazis called it. My grandparents wore one. But Peter and I, the Catholics in the family, did not have to.

Not that Catholics were spared persecution. The Nazis censored Catholic publications, shut down Catholic schools, confiscated Church properties, and deported over 2,500 priests to concentration camps.

Soon the casualties of the war touched me personally. Karli, my half-brother, was drafted into the German *Luftwaffe* (Air Force) and was shot down and killed in his Messerschmitt fighter plane over North Africa. The Russians forced Kotja's father into hard labor in a coal field in Ukraine, where he died under the cruel conditions, and Kotja's mother was banished to a labor camp in Siberia.

I noticed our Jewish neighbors in Berlin disappearing. One day they lived next door or down the street and the next day they were gone. That's what our neighbors must have thought about my mother after the day in March 1942, only six months after we had moved back with her in Berlin, the time when Peter and I turned the corner toward home and watched the Gestapo take her away.

Later the same month my mother was taken, after Peter and I had returned to Tante Irma's, my grandfather received a call-up notice from the Nazis ordering him to report to a train bound for the Theresienstadt ghetto in Czechoslovakia. That encampment was a holding pen for Jews on their way to either a forced-labor concentration camp or one of the new "killing centers" that the Nazis had opened.

Those killing centers—others called them death camps—were expressly designed for the mass murder of as many as 6,000 people per day in assembly-line fashion in gas chambers or by a firing squad's bullet through the back of their head. Their corpses were burned to ashes in ovens or bulldozed into vast pits.

My grandfather knew what had happened to his brothers-in-law and family business partners, Willy and Adolf Cohn, after they had reported to the trains with their call-up letters. They both died in death camps. So instead of taking that train to Theresienstadt, my grandfather swallowed a handful of pills and took his own life. Three months later my grandmother died, whether from a broken heart, at the hands of the Nazis, or from another cause, I never found out.

By the end of 1942, the Nazis had massacred over 1 million Jews, Gypsies, and Soviet prisoners at death camps in Belzec, Sobibor, Treblinka, and Auschwitz-Birkenau. I loved one of them. On Christmas Day, 1942, Tante Irma sat down with Peter and me. "I have something I need to tell you," she said. "Your mother has died in Auschwitz."

Chapter 6

SURVIVAL

I could spend hours telling you about the suffering the war has brought, but I'd only make myself more miserable. All we can do is wait, as calmly as possible, for it to end. Jews and Christians alike are waiting, the whole world is waiting, and many are waiting for death.

- Anne Frank, *The Diary of a Young Girl*

DANGAST, GERMANY, 1942-1944

HERR PILLE HAD informed Tante Irma in August that my mother had been killed in Auschwitz, but for some reason, Tante Irma waited until Christmas Day of 1942 to tell Peter and me. I cried. I felt numb. Was my father still alive? I could only hope so. My only comfort came in the assurance that Tante Irma loved me like her own son and would not abandon me.

Yes, I lived through difficult and very bad times, but as a kid, you put up with whatever happens. We didn't know anything different, we just lived our lives. We had to, we had no choice. We made the best of it.

I worried about my mother's apartment in Berlin. She left all of our entire family's possessions in the world in that apartment. I couldn't stand the thought of the Nazis ransacking our home. I had to find out if anything had happened to it.

I convinced Waltraud to take the train to Berlin with me one night and check out the apartment.

As we step off the train the sirens blast their air-raid warning. We dash into the *Luftschutzraum* (air defense room) at the train station and wait for the Allied bombers to pass. We sit for hours until the *"Entwarnung"* ("all clear") sign flashes on.

We come up from the bunker into a city on fire. Perfect timing! The mayhem gives us cover for our covert mission. But how will we get to my mother's apartment miles away on the other side of the city? We start walking, flames shoot at us from burning buildings on both sides. We dodge the bricks and concrete and boards and glass and furniture and shingles flying through the air out of the crumbling homes, stores, and offices. We smell the burnt rubber, and smoke and ash sting our eyes, noses, and throats. We feel the asphalt melting under our feet.

A Jeep with two German soldiers plows through the wreckage toward us. *We're caught. It's over.* There's nowhere to go. If we run, they'll shoot us. The soldiers pull in front of us and grill us: "What are you people doing? Where are you going?"

"We're going to our friend's apartment," Waltraud says, and tells them my mother's address.

By now they've had a good glimpse at tall, blonde, beautiful Waltraud, and their tone softens.

"Jump in, we'll take you." They are so enchanted by Waltraud that they pay no attention to the eleven-year-old Jewish boy next to her.

It's a miracle that my mother's building has not collapsed or burned down and that only one side is damaged.

I recovered my grandfather's model of Sinding's Valkyrie from my mother's apartment in Berlin. A piece of her arm broke off in one of the bombings.

Waltraud and I read the Nazis "RESTRICTED AREA. NO TRESPASSING. CIVILIANS WILL BE EXECUTED" seal across the door and glance at each other. I rip off the seal and toss it in the rubble.

I open the door and there's everything just as I remembered—my grandparents' living room furniture and pieces of art, my mother's bedroom set and personal belongings, the Hedy Lamarr home movies, photographs, and other personal papers my mother saved, including my grandfather's World War I Iron Cross for bravery and heroism certificate.

I can't leave anything behind for the Royal Air Force to bomb or the Nazis to plunder. Waltraud and I try to find a way to move it all to Irmenfried, and after three days—three days during which we might have been discovered and shot—we find someone with a van willing to take my family's belongings to Dangast.

"It was perfectly normal"

Air raids seemed perfectly normal to Waltraud, me, and everyone at Irmenfried. Planes by the hundreds and thousands constantly barreled toward Berlin. The engines roared like thunder and shook the air and the ground. For defense, the German Navy deployed fog machines on barges in the North Sea. Drums on the barges released chlorosulfuric acid, which attracted moisture and created artificial fog—a smoke screen—which hid not only the naval base but also the village of Dangast from the pilots.

The German Navy also stationed anti-aircraft artillery about ten miles away from Irmenfried at Wilhelmshaven, the largest German naval base, and we watched the spotlights and explosions light up the sky above our heads over 50 times throughout the war.

When the anti-aircraft missiles blew up a plane, shrapnel flew everywhere, and often some landed on our campground. We made a game of it. We'd guess whether a piece came from the plane's top or bottom or side, and trade pieces like baseball cards. Scraps with letters or insignia on them were the most in demand. We were kids, and even in the middle of a war, we found ways to have fun, and that helped us survive.

One day I found a flare that pilots use after they're shot down to show their squadron where they are. *I'm going to light it and see what it looks like up close.* I stuck the flare in a slot in our monkey bars, lit the fuse, and *BOOM,* the sparks blinded me for three days and scarred my cheek for life.

On another afternoon I was riding bikes in the countryside with a group of kids and an Allied fighter plane slowed down and shot at us. We crashed our bikes into the *Einmannlocher* (one-man-holes) dug along the side of the road to hide and the plane flew by. None of us was hurt but we wrecked our bikes.

Another day while I was out on the shrimp boat a dogfight broke out over our heads between American and German fighter planes. An American plane got hit and spiraled toward the sea. The pilot ejected and we watched him parachute into the ice-cold water. We pulled in our nets, fired up our engines, and soared off on a search and rescue mission.

We found the pilot, a Canadian, still afloat, and shivering from hypothermia. We pulled him onto our boat and I took him below to the cabin. He didn't speak any German and I spoke no English, but as I helped him get into dry clothes, wrapped him in a blanket, lit a warm fire, fixed him a hot cup of coffee and something to eat, words weren't necessary for us to bond as friends.

He stayed with us the entire day but the Germans were waiting for him when we returned to the harbor and hauled him away as a prisoner of war.

Bunker Down

Herr Pille knew the Allied air raids would become more frequent and more deadly, and organized the bigger kids in the village to build our own bomb shelter behind the schoolhouse. He had no blueprint or drawings to go by so we just shoveled out a big hole.

To build the walls, roof, and benches, we gathered stray planks from the wooden bridges and piers on the North Sea that had been busted off by the icy tide and drifted to the beach. We bundled and tied the planks together and hitched them to a team of horses that dragged them back to the schoolhouse. We spread dirt over the roof for camouflage.

It took us months to finish the shelter, and we got plenty of use out of it. When we heard the air raid sirens blare we'd bolt from our classrooms, run full speed to the bunker, and huddle underground. If a bomb were to fall right on top of us, we'd be gone, but if it exploded miles away, we wouldn't be killed or injured by the shrapnel, so our homemade bunker was better than nothing.

Circled are me (left), Peter, and Herr Pille with our classmates digging our bomb shelter
Photo credit: "From Danagst to Colorado Springs," by Gert Groning

Our German classmates hated the Allied air raids, but Peter and I—the two Austrian Jews hiding from the Nazis—inwardly cheered *ZUKOMMEN! ZUKOMMEN!* (Come on! Come on!) during every one. We hated everything to do with Hitler and wanted more air raids so the Germans would be defeated sooner.

We bunkered down during a raid until we heard the "all clear" signal—usually about 45 minutes or an hour later. Then we'd walk back to class as if nothing had happened.

Not all of the action happened in the air. While I was steering the fishing boat one foggy night a gray monstrosity popped out of the water next to me. I could only gawk and yell to Captain Blanke and my mate who were sleeping below deck. "You've got to come and see this!"

It was a German *Unterseeboot* (undersea boat, or U-Boat, a submarine) on its way back to the Wilhelmshaven naval base, maybe from a torpedo run or maybe from a test drive since they built U-Boats at the base. If that steel beast

SURVIVAL

had surfaced 30 yards to the starboard side it would have snapped our boat in half like a toothpick and not even realized we were in its path.

"We were always hungry"

Food, clothing, and other necessities had been scarce since Hitler invaded Austria and Poland, but now, with America, Great Britain, Russia, and all the Allied forces attacking Germany, the Nazis issued strict food rationing cards that allowed Tante Irma to buy only a half-pound of meat per week and a half-pound of butter per month.

We continued to grow as much as we could in our gardens, and it helped that I worked on fishing boats because I always had a meal to bring home, but still, we were always hungry. We did what we had to do to survive, and sometimes that meant stuffing our pockets with potatoes and apples from a neighbor's farm.

С Рождеством

On the farms in the village, we worked alongside prisoners of war from Russia and Serbia who were held at *Dulag Nord 43* (transit camp north #43) on the Wilhelmshaven naval base.

The POWs were friendly, and one of the Russians "adopted" me because I reminded him of his sons waiting for him back home. It's amazing how our friendship developed without speaking the same language!

One Christmas Tante Irma and I knocked on the prison *Kommandant's* (commander's) office door and asked if we could invite my Russian friend and his buddy to Christmas dinner. The commander had been around Dangast for so long that he recognized and trusted us, and he wasn't SS or Gestapo so he wasn't hunting down Jews.

"Of course," the commander said. And it was a *С Рождеством* (Merry Christmas) for all.

The most abundant source of food was off-limits. The German Army had hijacked a large house in Dangast and turned it into a *Logierhaus* (lodging house) for soldiers. Exploring the village one day, a group of us peeked in the kitchen windows and salivated. *Boy, if we could just get some of that food!* We asked the soldiers but they wouldn't give us even a piece of bread.

So Peter and I take matters into our own hands. We sneak over to the lodging house in the middle of the night and spot crates stacked with sacks of flour near the kitchen door. We crawl up to the door on our bellies, open it, and inch one of the crates outside.

We've nudged the crate about twenty yards from the house and past a tree when a soldier walks through the kitchen and out the door directly toward us. *Does he see us? Probably not, it's pitch dark. Should we run? No, he wouldn't kill us for taking flour.* We lie still next to the crate and hold our breath as the soldier comes closer and closer. Then he stops at the tree, relieves himself, and turns to go back inside. *Puh, das war nah!!!* (Whew, that was close!!!)

It took us a couple of hours to push the crate home, and we feasted on bread and pasta for weeks.

Stealing is never a good thing, but we stole to stay alive.

We didn't have a lot of clothes either. No one could buy new clothes in Germany during the war. One year when we outgrew our shoes the only kind Tante Irma found were wooden clogs from Holland. After some practice, we learned how to run in them. In the winter we stuffed them with hay to keep our feet warm.

The Allies dropped 68,000 tons of bombs on Berlin. The destruction killed thousands of people and displaced almost 2 million Berliners. It's a miracle that none of the bombs landed on us.

Chapter 7

LIBERATION

This is the day. The invasion has begun. Is this really the beginning of the long-awaited liberation? The liberation we've all talked so much about, which still seems too good, too much of a fairy tale ever to come true? Will this year, 1944, bring us victory? We don't know yet. But where there's hope, there's life. It fills us with fresh courage and makes us strong again.

- Anne Frank, *The Diary of a Young Girl*

DANGAST, GERMANY, 1944-1946

YES, THE BOMBINGS and supply shortages made everything difficult, but we didn't stop living our lives.

In 1944, Waltraud received a marriage proposal from a German Army soldier and SS officer named Willy Hinck. When they broke the news to me, I did what any love-struck twelve-year-old boy would do. I challenged Willy to a duel. With real pistols. Never mind that he was an SS officer.

"Whoever wins can marry Waltraud," I said.

Willy just grinned at me.

"What are you smiling about? I'm serious," I said.

"I'll talk to Waltraud about it," Willy said.

The duel never happened. Herr Pille officiated Waltraud's wedding, and the newlyweds moved to Varel, a larger town about five miles away.

The constant air raids over Europe canceled the Summer Olympic games scheduled in London but didn't stop the Hitler Youth Olympics of 1944 in Dangast.

I posted my best Youth Olympics performance ever in the hand grenade throw. They scored our throws on a combination of distance and accuracy. I launched my grenade 45 meters, which is about 50 yards, and straight enough for second place.

I saved my certificate, which I was proud of except for two things: the swastika printed at the top, and the misspelling of my name.

The date on the certificate, May 14, 1944, is about a month shy of my twelfth birthday, and 23 days before the turning point of the war—D-Day, the day of the Allied invasion and liberation of Normandy, France, on June 6. Peter and I first heard about D-Day from villagers in Dangast. Just as Anne Frank—a Jewish teenager in hiding 200 miles from us in Amsterdam—wrote in her diary, the D-Day news filled Peter and me with "hope, life, and fresh courage."

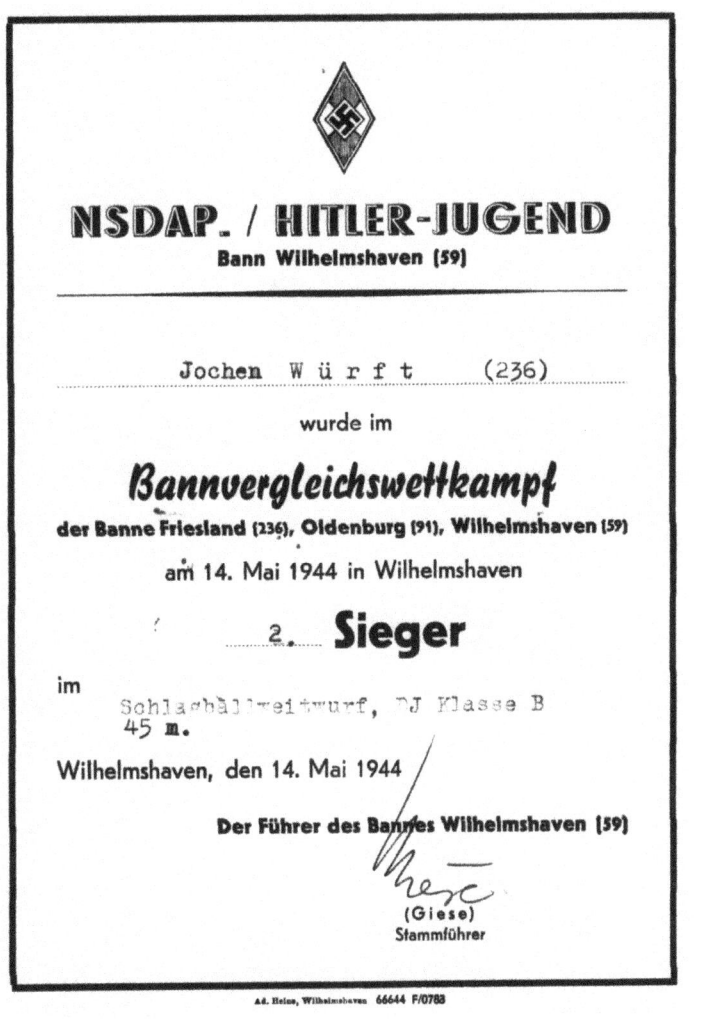

Second place in the youth olympics grenade throw!

Our optimism spiked again in August when the Allies liberated Paris, and we knew that in a matter of time they would march into Germany. The next spring, in May 1945, Dangast lit up with chatter about what had happened to Hitler because he stopped making public addresses. Where was Hitler? Soon the truth reached us that he had committed suicide.

LIBERATION

Chocolate Bars

Shortly after Hitler's suicide, a division of the German Army marched into Dangast and conscripted villagers of all ages, including Kotja, Peter, me, into the *Volkssturm* (people's storm) which was the civilian fighting force. The soldiers handed us shovels, rifles, and hand grenades and ordered us to dig foxholes in the fields and hold off the oncoming American troops while they retreated to the North Sea.

I'm thirteen years old and you want me to hold off the Americans?

I dug my hole and knew how to fire a rifle and toss a grenade but no way I was going to shoot at the Americans.

All of a sudden, down the hill rolled a convoy of trucks. I could tell it was the U.S. Army coming at us because the hoods weren't long like on German trucks. But they were flying white flags! When they saw us in the fields, they stopped their trucks and walked toward us. We jumped out of our holes, ran to them, and they tried to explain what was going on. We didn't understand enough English to comprehend but we understood that the chocolate bars they handed us meant the war was over! Indeed, Germany had surrendered on May 7, 1945.

The American convoy continued its advance to the North Sea, where the German Army surrendered.

"The Canadian soldiers were great to us"

The atmosphere changed completely around Dangast when the Royal Canadian occupation troops entered the village and took over all the Nazi properties in the village. I'll never forget the first English words that Tante Irma taught me: "I live in the white house in the Canadian camp." She instructed me to tell that to every Canadian soldier I met so maybe they would help their neighbor.

Her strategy worked! The Canadian soldiers were great to us. They used the kitchen in the house where we had stolen flour from the Germans to cook for their troops and brought all the leftovers to us. Some nights we overflowed with food and invited friends for dinner. Everything tasted delicious, and what a blessing to have occasional days when I did not feel hungry.

In return, all the Canadians wanted from us were Nazi souvenirs, especially

We traded memorabilia for cash and food with the Canadian soldiers
Photo credit: Wikimedia Commons

the various pins that the Nazis had issued to civilians every month. I had dozens of Hitler Youth membership badges and sports badges, and the Canadians went crazy over pins and patches with a swastika. We traded the memorabilia for cigarettes and then sold the cigarettes in Berlin and made a lot of money.

The Canadians also wanted German watches and cameras—the Leicas and Hasselblads—so we'd buy them with our cigarette profits and sell or trade them with the soldiers. Tante Irma also got in on the wheeling and dealing. She earned cash, food, and supplies by washing soldiers' laundry.

We welcomed the occupation troops. They were rescuing us; they were rescuing Germany.

But did anyone rescue my father? I hadn't seen him for several years. I heard nothing from him or about him. Was he even still alive?

Goodbye, Good Friends

There was a downside to the Canadian occupation. I lost two friends.

Herr Pille was arrested and sent to a prison in Varel.

Heiko, Herr Pille's youngest son and my best friend, was playing with some other boys one afternoon in the air raid bunkers at the Wilhelmshaven naval base. Why I didn't go with them I don't remember, but it was the day when the Canadians blew up the anti-aircraft battery at the base. A cloud of falling concrete crushed Heiko to death. We had been so lucky to live through the war together, and now he was dead. I've never stopped grieving for him.

Population Boom

We were fortunate that the Canadians were so generous because immediately after the war the food shortages grew worse than they were during the war. The German economy collapsed. Factories, farms, stores, offices, and homes were mostly bombed out of existence. At my beloved Berlin Zoo, only 91 of over 4,000 animals survived.

At the Yalta Conference, the Allied leaders divided Germany into eastern and western occupation zones. Over a million people in eastern Germany fled in our direction to the west to escape the harsh Russian occupation. The population of Dangast doubled, and the Allied authorities required every household to take in refugees and give them food and a place to sleep. A nice family that had evacuated Berlin lived at Tante Irma's with us.

With more people and less food, we had to work harder and smarter. We ate fewer vegetables and more plants. We stretched our spinach with weeds. Meat was scarce. Once in a while, Tante Irma would buy horse meat, but our main source was the 40 to 50 rabbits we raised in wooden cages behind the house.

Feeding that many rabbits was a major task. Every day Peter, Kotja, and I each picked a sackful of dandelions for them. We ate rabbit once a week for Sunday dinner—one rabbit sliced up for the entire family—and it was my job to prepare a fat one every Saturday. I got so efficient that I could kill it, skin it, cut it open, and have it in the pot ready for cooking in eight minutes!

I'd hang the rabbit skin to dry and Tante Irma would make gloves, scarves, hats, and shoe linings for us out of the fur.

A consequence of scavenging for food was an outbreak of food poisoning throughout Irmenfried and Dangast. Kotja, Peter, me, and most of the kids at school all had big bumps on our legs that oozed greenish-yellowish pus down to our ankles. The bumps felt like they were on fire but we had to keep up with our chores to keep eating. Tante Irma wrapped our legs with wegerich plant leaves, an anti-inflammatory herb. The wegerich brought relief, but it took about a year for the infection to completely clear up.

I also continued to work on the farms and the fishing boats while Peter focused on selling and trading with the Canadian soldiers. Still, if we didn't have Canadian leftovers we didn't always know where our next meal was coming from.

In 1946, Peter enrolled in a school about 30 miles away in the city of Oldenburg. There he met Alan Hill, an English colonel who worked for the United Nations. Peter asked Colonel Hill if there was any way for Peter and me to emigrate to America.

Chapter 8

DISPLACED

The sun is shining, the sky is deep blue, there's a magnificent breeze and I'm longing — really longing — for everything: conversation, freedom, friends.

- Anne Frank, *The Diary of a Young Girl*

DANGAST, GERMANY, 1946-1950

PETER AND I were tired of Germany. The Nazis had killed our family. Life was grueling during the war and it wasn't much easier after the war. Seven years in hiding wore us out and we wanted to get away to someplace peaceful and free.

Colonel Hill recommended that Peter and I apply for relocation to America through the United States Committee for the Care of European Children (USCOM), an organization of Jewish and Catholic groups that helped place children under eighteen years of age. We applied right away, but so did hundreds of thousands of other children throughout Europe.

We also contacted our father's brothers in Ecuador. They sent us food and supplies and invited us to come and live with them. We applied for visas, but so did millions of other people throughout Europe and the heap of paperwork bogged down the process to a snail's pace.

After jumping through hoops for a year we finally received approval, our papers, and reservations on a boat to Ecuador—just in time for their new dictator to change the constitution, which rendered our visas null and void.

Stuck in Germany and now graduated from eighth grade, I worked full-time to help feed our family and the refugee guests from Berlin. But I also found time for new adventures.

Hell's Valley

As much as we loved the North Sea, Peter and I missed the hills and mountains that we had hiked so many times as young boys. So one day we decided to make an expedition to the Austrian border and climb the Zugspitze, the highest peak in the Austrian-German Alps at 9,718 feet and home to three glaciers.

It was also 500 miles away. We packed our jackets, extra clothes and underwear, and set out for the border via the only reliable form of transportation operating in Germany at the time—we hitch-hiked. Ten rides and seven days later, we arrived at base camp on the German side of the mountain. After another night sleeping under the stars—one night in an apple orchard—we woke up at 5 am to begin our ascent.

There are a few different routes to climb Zugspitze, each with a different degree of difficulty. We chose the Höllentalklamm Gorge, which is the most difficult. It's not called *Höllentalklamm* (Hell's Valley) for nothing. Why did we pick the most difficult route? Because I was fourteen and Peter was turning sixteen.

We had no hiking boots, no spikes, no ropes or harnesses, and no climbing gear of any kind.

As other climbers crossed our path on their way down they would ask us, "Boys, where are you going?"

"To the top," we'd answer.

"You can't do that! You don't have the right equipment. Do you know what you're doing? My God, you'll never make it!" One professional climber was at least kind enough to give us a rope after he berated us.

While climbing one of the glaciers we reached a point where we stopped and stared up at a five-foot gap between the glacier and a rock wall above us on the mountain, and stared down at the gorge thousands of feet below. I was scared to death but had no choice but to jump, grab onto the wall and pull myself up onto the mountain.

All I can say is that we both made the jump and reached the summit by 9 pm—a total miracle. We beheld the beauty of the Alps, the glacier, the waterfall, and the gorge, then hiked over to the *Schneefernerhaus* (snow distant house) at the top of the mountain. That was the lodge at the top of the mountain where climbers could have a meal and sleep in a warm cot before descending. The next morning, Peter and I descended on the Austrian side.

When my feet were firmly planted on flat ground at the base of Zugspitze I told Peter, "I'm glad we did it, but I'll never climb another mountain. Never." I've tried a lot of daring feats in my life, but mountain climbing? Way too scary.

Canadian Thanksgiving

Later in 1946, another miracle appeared at my front door. I heard a knock, opened the door, and we recognized each other immediately—me and the Canadian pilot I helped fish out of the North Sea a few years before. We shook hands and he gave me a hug. After a few years in a German POW camp, he learned enough German to tell me that his name was Gerald Gleison from London, Ontario, and to thank me for saving his life.

I'm glad I climbed the Zugspitze, but I'll never climb another mountain
Photoc credit: Huber Photo

While Gerald stayed with us in Dangast, Tante Irma served as our interpreter since she had learned English when she worked in a nursery in England before opening Irmenfried. He explained that he came back to Dangast after his release to thank the fishing crew that rescued him. He found Captain Blanke at the harbor and Blanke gave Gerald my name and address.

We took a long walk along the dike of the North Sea one day and talked about our experiences during the war and our hopes and dreams for the future. He stopped and carved his name and hometown into the wood of one of the gates lining a cow pasture along the dike.

Gerald visited for a few days, then said goodbye. I appreciated his effort to find me and thank me. I've thought about him often but never saw him again.

The Apprentice

Life didn't get better in Germany until 1948 when the United States implemented the Marshall Plan, which pumped $11 billion into Europe's economies. Rationing limits were relaxed and we could buy butter and sugar and cornbread and real coffee beans and pies and everything else we needed.

With more food available, Tante Irma didn't need the fish and shrimp I brought home, so she steered me toward another career—landscaping. She introduced me to Herr G. H. Brauer at the Brauer Nurseries about ten miles away in Grünenkamp. He offered me a landscaping apprenticeship and I accepted.

I rode my bike to Grünenkamp on Monday mornings, lived at the nursery all week, and pedaled back to Irmenfried on Friday afternoons. Between the apprenticeship and Tante Irma's tutoring, I learned everything there is to know about azaleas and rhododendrons and memorized the botanical names of most trees and bushes.

"Go out and do the best you can"

By November 1949, at age seventeen, I was on my way to a career as a landscape gardener, following in Tante Irma's footsteps, when a representative of the U.S. Army at a base in southern Germany called Peter and me.

"Boys, we just found your records," the officer said. "We know about your father working in the Austrian government and that your mother was killed in Auschwitz. We are now familiar with your story, and if you would like to come to America, we are more than happy to have you. The United States Committee for the Care of European Children is ready to make the arrangements."

"But we have no visas or immigration papers," we said.

"You're considered victims of fascism, so you can leave right away. USCOM has a place in New York City where you can stay until your papers arrive," the officer said.

When we told Tante Irma, she cried tears of both joy and sadness. "You're my children," she said, "and I will miss you terribly. But go. You're going to paradise. Go out and taste the world and do the best you can."

It hurt to say goodbye to Kotja, but I brightened up when he said, "I'll follow you someday."

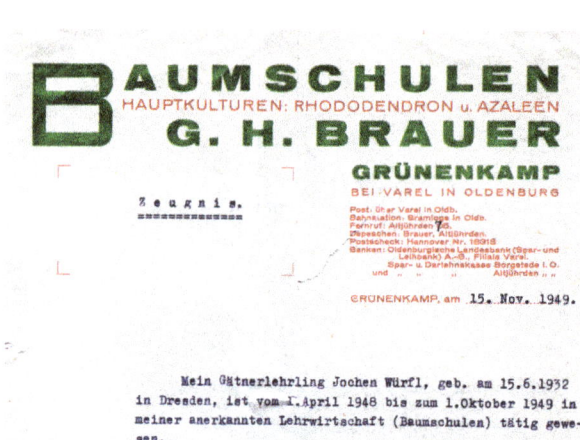

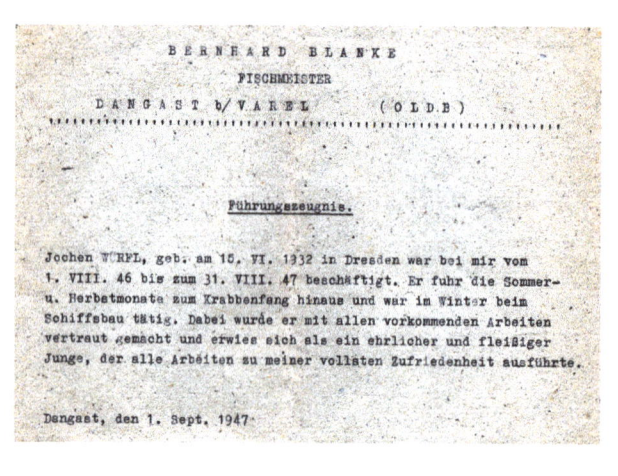

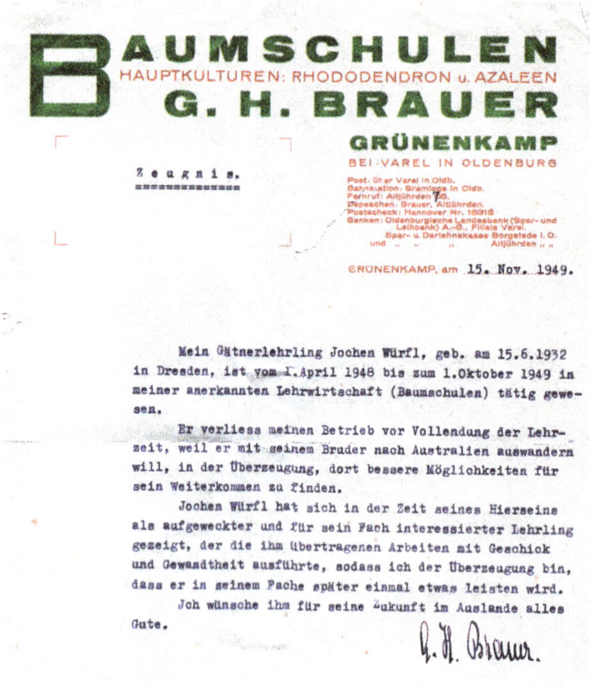

My letters of recommendation from Bauer Nurseries (top) and Captain Blanke

"I'll help you," I promised.

I gave notice to Herr Brauer at the nursery and said goodbye to Captain Blanke down at the docks. Both of them wrote letters of recommendation for me to show potential employers when I looked for a job in America.

Within a few weeks, Peter and I packed one bag of belongings each and left on the first leg of our journey—to a "displaced persons" camp run by the U.S. Army in Verden, about 75 miles from Dangast.

The camp teemed with thousands of children and was not very pleasant. The rooms were overcrowded and the beds were lumpy, but I had nothing to complain about. I would soon be liberated from Germany.

I was fortunate because not every hidden child's story had a happy ending, including Anne Frank's. Anne and her family were discovered and arrested by the Nazis two months after D-Day. Anne was deported to Auschwitz in a cattle wagon and later transferred to the Bergen-Belsen concentration camp. She died about six months afterward from the typhus epidemic that ravaged the camp.

To pass the time at Verden I played games with the other boys and girls and met a lot of nice kids. I buddied around most days with a fourteen-year-old girl named Garmia who was by herself at the camp. She called me Johan

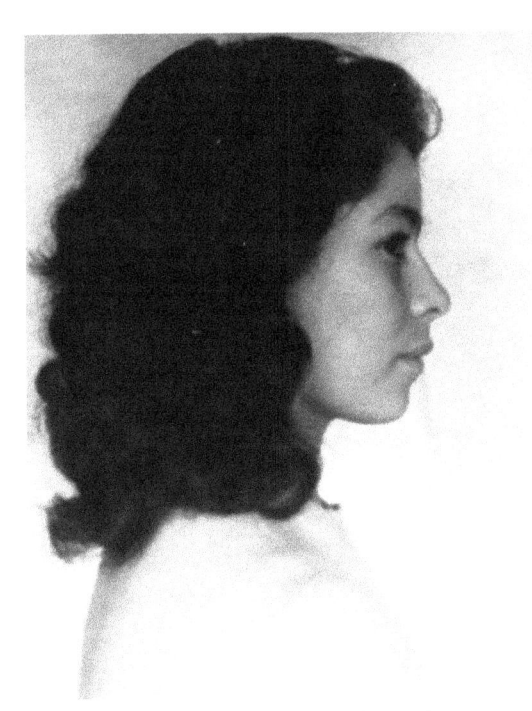

My friend Garmia from the displaced persons camp in Verden

because she couldn't pronounce Jochen, and nicknamed me "little brother." I still have her picture that she gave me.

In December 1944 USCOM moved Peter, me, and more than 50 other kids headed for America to Klingberg, Germany, about 170 miles from Dangast. We lived in beautiful houses with plenty of room—much nicer than jam-packed Verden.

We celebrated Christmas, which made me miss Tante Irma and her Christmas room. But I could only think of America when on January 1, 1950, Peter and I boarded a Scandinavian Airlines plane at the Bremen, Germany, airport.

I was so happy when the pilot announced we were on our way to New York City, I couldn't believe it. I was seventeen, on a plane for the first time in my life, and taking off to a new life in America.

MY SECOND LIFE
1950 - PRESENT

America, to me, is freedom.
Willie Nelson

Chapter 9

FREEDOM

NEW YORK, USA, 1950

WE FLEW IN a four-engine, four-propeller plane from Bremen to Scotland, where we refueled before crossing the Atlantic Ocean to Halifax, Canada. I had watched thousands and thousands of planes fly over Dangast, and now I felt such a rush riding in one that I thought, *I'm going to become a pilot someday.*

Somewhere above the Atlantic, I noticed the passengers on one side of the plane with their eyes wide open staring out the window. I looked out and my eyes popped when I saw that one of the propellers wasn't spinning, which meant that one of our engines had conked out.

"This is your captain speaking," we heard over the loudspeaker. "Relax. There's nothing to worry about. We've made this trip many times on three engines."

Relax? Nothing to worry about?

As we approached Canada we couldn't see much of anything out the windows anymore because we were flying into a blinding blizzard. *So, for years I watched bombers get shot out of the sky during a war. Now I'm riding in a passenger plane for the first time in my life and we're flying through a blizzard and missing an engine. Will this plane spiral into the Atlantic like those bombers that dropped into the North Sea?*

"We've done this before. We'll be okay," the captain reassured us. And he was right. We landed safely in Halifax on the morning of January 2.

The mechanics went to work on the dead engine and the airport officials moved the passengers into a hangar and brought us food and blankets. When they announced that the repairs would not be finished until the next day, they brought us cots to sleep on.

NEW YORK, NEW YORK

On January 3, 1950, Peter and I landed at LaGuardia Airport. I was so grateful to be in America. There were no black-uniformed agents to hunt me down, stop me on the street and ask me for identification and drag me away to die.

A USCOM bus took our group of about 35 kids to our dormitory in the Bronx. Just imagine growing up in a little village in a foreign country and all of a sudden you're riding a bus in downtown New York City. I saw skyscrapers for the first time in my life, but what captivated me most were the hundreds, thousands, maybe millions of cars everywhere as far as my eyes could see. I had never seen so many cars in all my life. Big cars. Packards and Hudsons and Nashes and Studebakers.

My first thought was, *I'm here, and I'm going to do everything I can to succeed in this country, to do something, to build something. And someday I'm going to drive a car like one of these.*

My biggest fear was that there would not be enough work in this world for me to do.

The bus pulled up to our dorm, a large rectangular building on Bryant Avenue in the Hunts Point area of the Bronx—not a highrise, but too many rooms to be one family's house. We were in a poorer neighborhood. The building was clean and nice but stark—nothing fancy.

A Jewish man in his mid-thirties and his girlfriend, both native New Yorkers, lived in the building and managed everything. The two of them, and a few other men they supervised, took care of us.

The first thing they did was hand out new clothes to all of us—pants, shirts, winter coats, hats, gloves, and everything else we needed. They gave every boy and girl the same clothes so we all looked the same.

Then they assigned us to our rooms—four or five to a room, boys on one side of the building, girls on the other. Peter and I roomed together. One of our roommates came from Yugoslavia with his sister. Out of our window, at a distance, we watched the planes taking off and landing at LaGuardia. I slept fine in a comfortable bed.

The kids and the native New Yorkers in the dorm all had trouble with my first name. No one could pronounce *Jochen* so they called me *Johnny*. I hated *Johnny*, but it was too late.

I don't know the history of the building but it contained a synagogue. The rabbi would catch up with some of us on Fridays and ask us to turn on the lights in the synagogue and set up for Sabbath services. He didn't ask if any of us were Jewish so that didn't matter to him. The first time I turned on the lights was the first time I remember ever stepping into a synagogue.

On my third day in New York, our hosts took us on a tour to the top of the Empire State Building, the Statue of Liberty, the Rainbow Room at Rockefeller Center, Wall Street, Times Square—all the popular tourist spots. In Times Square, Peter, our roommate, and I stopped in one of those photo booths where you pick the background setting and they take your picture. Of course, I wanted the car.

We learned how to navigate the subway system, and we explored New York on our own every day. With a dollar in our pocket courtesy of USCOM, we were on our way to the Central Park Zoo, Long Island, Chinatown, Little Italy, the Russian neighborhood, and the Ukrainian neighborhood—we were unleashed to go anywhere and do anything we wanted, and I reveled in my newfound freedom.

As a kid used to mountains and hills and beaches, rambling around a big city twice the size of Berlin showed me how different the world is and how

My third day in New York City with Peter (far left) and a roommate (middle) from the USCOM house

FREEDOM

55

much more there is to see, and sparked my love for traveling.

We were not allowed to attend school because USCOM was waiting for our immigration papers to come through so technically we were illegal aliens. But we took English classes in the dorm and learned enough to get by in the city.

I was in heaven at the New York Public Library learning about the Declaration of Independence and the Constitution. America stood for everything that Germany had stood against. I wanted to find out why America is so different, and why people have so much freedom, which was unheard of in Europe when I grew up.

I wanted to be ready to find a place to live and a job once my papers arrived, so at the library, I read all I could about the states and cities in America. Chicago, New Orleans, Miami—so many places appealed to me. But I set my heart on a city on the water that looked beautiful in the pictures and was home to an international population—San Francisco. I told Peter how much I thought we would like it there and he agreed to go as soon as we could.

Every day I hoped that our papers would come. I had no idea it would take so long, but it was okay because I was in New York. I was out of Germany.

In June, our immigration documents finally arrived and I was a completely free man. People who have never lived under a dictator—with no personal rights of any kind, and always told by the government what they could do and what they couldn't do—can't fully appreciate what it meant for me to come to this country and have the freedom to do anything I wanted. I was living a dream.

The Greyhound bus to...

By June, Peter had found a girlfriend, Elsa, a Latino girl originally from Panama. "You go ahead to San Francisco and I'll catch up with you later," he said. I had turned eighteen and was eager to start my new life in America so traveling by myself was fine with me.

People told me the cheapest way to travel in the U.S. was by Greyhound bus, so I took the subway to the bus terminal, handed the lady at the ticket counter all the money in my pocket, and said, "I need a ticket to San Francisco, please."

She counted my money and said, "You're going to need a lot more than this."

"That's all I have. How far can I go?"

"You can get to Baltimore."

"Is that on the way to San Francisco?" I asked.

"It's in the right direction," she said.

"I'll be back."

I went home and told Peter I was going only to Baltimore, not all the way to San Francisco. "I'll go with you then," he said, "and see what it's like."

A few days later we stepped off the bus on Centre Street in downtown Baltimore. Across from the bus terminal, I spotted the sign for an employment agency run by the State of Maryland. We walked in and explained that we just arrived from New York and were looking for jobs.

"What is your name?" the man asked me.

"My name is Jack."

Author's Note:
The Wall Street Journal, January 3, 1950

Image used with permission from the Wall Street Journal

One of my favorite gifts was a "rare document of the past," an original issue of the *Wall Street Journal* from the day I arrived in America. There are twenty pages in the entire newspaper, which cost 10 cents.

The news of the day included congress's plans to ease the displaced persons law:

High on the list of Democratic legislative goals are an expanded social security program, repeal of the margarine taxes, liberalization of the displaced persons law, federal funds for education, and civil rights measures

Production records continue to be shattered by the young television industry. November's record output of 414,223 sets was almost double the year-earlier total

FM Station Death Rate Up; Television Boom Is a Factor

Royal Typewriter Company reported the highest sales of portable typewriters in the company's history

The price of Brazil's famous beverage coffee beans rose to over 50 cents a pound, compared to 28 cents in 1948

Worsted Wool suits from the London Shop were advertised on sale for $64.50

The Dow Jones Industrial Average closed at 200.13

Chapter 10

WINGS AND ROOTS

BALTIMORE, MARYLAND, USA, 1950-1952

I HATED WHEN people called me Johnny, but what did I want to be called? I thought long and hard and…why not Jack? It flowed naturally from Jochen and Johnny but sounded better to me. Everyone I've met since I moved to Baltimore knows me as Jack, starting with the gentleman at the employment agency across from the bus terminal.

He was very friendly and helpful and even spoke a little German. He flipped through his Rolodex, made a few phone calls, and called me back over to his desk.

"Well, I have one job for you. It's at Miller's Tie Factory on South Paca Street not far from here. You can report for work tomorrow morning if you want."

"Danke schön!" I said. ("Thank you very much!")

He also found a job for Peter at a trouser factory in Highlandtown.

Our next task was to find a place to live.

While walking around downtown searching for a place, Peter and I stopped to admire the Basilica on Cathedral Street. I noticed the Catholic Archdiocese brick building next to it. I rang the doorbell and a gentleman named Mr. Libertini opened the door. I explained how my brother and I came to America from Germany through USCOM, which is run by Catholic and Jewish groups, and that we were looking for a place to sleep.

Mr. Libertini seemed to be familiar with USCOM and said, "Yeah, I think I can find something for you." He called the nuns at St. Mary's Seminary a few blocks away on Paca Street. The dorms were empty because the seminarians were away for the summer and they let us stay in one. I couldn't have asked for anything better! I could walk to my job!

I'll never forget Mr. Libertini. He treated me to dinner one night and I drank a cold concoction I had never seen in my life—ice cream mixed with milk and syrup—a chocolate milkshake! He called me every so often to find out if I needed anything, and I'd run into him downtown once in a while.

My job at the necktie factory was very important. I arrived at 7 am, went down to the basement, and turned on the steam pipes so that the ladies on the fourth floor had steam to iron the ties before they were shipped out to the stores. After I turned on the steam I swept the factory floors, cleaned the bathrooms, and helped pack orders.

Four Jewish brothers owned the factory and they were happy that they could help me get on my feet in Baltimore. They paid me $20 a week, which combined with Peter's pay was enough to rent an apartment of our own on Mt. Royal Avenue.

I liked the 30 or 40 women who worked at the factory, and they were so kind to me. They knew I had just arrived in America and tried to make me feel welcome. Some of them invited me over for dinner. Others tried to fix me up with their daughters.

ENGLISH 1, 2, 3 AND 4

Next on my to-do list was learning more English and continuing my education, which I had stopped at eighth grade in Germany. My parents and Tante Irma impressed on me the importance of education so I wanted to go on to high school and college.

Since I worked full-time I needed to take classes at night. Co-workers told me that Baltimore City College High School (aka "City") offered night classes for adults. The night program fit my schedule, and the school wasn't far from work and home, so I enrolled.

City taught English levels 1, 2, 3, and 4, designed for students to take in sequence over four years. I couldn't wait that long so I signed up for all four levels in my first year and took one English class each night, Monday through Thursday.

For the first couple of months, I didn't understand much English at all. That made not only school tough, but also eating dinner. I only had two hours to eat and dash to class after work, not enough time to go home and cook so I'd stop at restaurants on the way to school.

But I didn't know how to order because I couldn't read most of the menu. All I recognized at first were fried eggs and milkshakes. You wouldn't believe how many eggs and shakes I ate until I learned how to order something else.

By Christmas, the English words started coming to me, and soon I could hold full and fluent conversations in English.

It took me a while to catch up with my classmates in English, but I outdid them in geography. People would ask me, "Where are you from?"

"Austria," I'd say.

"Oh, I'd love to visit there someday," they'd say. "Kangaroos are so cute."

"Not Australia," I'd say, "*Austria*."

"That's different?"

"Yeah, it's a different country."

"Where is it?"

FRIENDS

I made a best friend at school, Ben Parades. Ben came from El Salvador to work at their consulate in Baltimore and was in one of my English classes.

On weekends we'd try to meet other guys and girls at dances at the Alcazar Hotel and Ballroom. The bands didn't play waltzes in the 1950s so I had to learn new dances, like the swing and the jitterbug. Ben and I would also go to dances at the Dixie Ballroom at Gwynn Oak Park. Usually, we'd go to the park early and ride the rollercoasters before the dances started.

I'm glad I made friends because Peter hated his job, quit, and moved back to New York. "I've had enough of this hick town," he said. "I'll find a job and a place for us and then you can move back too," he suggested. I just shrugged.

Now on my own, I found a lower-cost room on North Calvert Street in a large house owned by an elderly lady who rented out all of her bedrooms. Not only was the price right, but I also gained seven nice guys as housemates, mostly dental students at the University of Maryland School of Dentistry. Every morning the lady fixed breakfast for us and packed us brown-bag lunches—all included in the rent.

One of the guys owned a car and offered to teach me how to drive. It took me a few outings to get the hang of working the clutch and the stick shift, but soon I was ready for my driving test and passed on my first try.

My social and civic network widened in December 1950 when a friend invited me to the "Sunday Evening Club" at the First Methodist Church downtown on Mount Vernon Place. The club brought in dinner speakers over a meal followed by a lively discussion.

One hot discussion topic was the civil war in Korea. Communist North Korea invaded democratic South Korea in June 1950, and America immediately entered the war in alliance with South Korea to stop the spread of communism.

U.S. General Douglas MacArthur said that American troops would be home by Christmas. When that didn't happen, public support for the war waned, which sparked spirited discussions about what America's role should be.

I met a gentleman at the club named Cal Jones, who owned the Baltimore Stationery Company. I told him about my job at Miller's Tie Factory and that I wanted a bigger challenge. He said, "Your English is good enough now that I don't think you'd have any problem finding a job in an office somewhere. Maybe I can help you because I sell office furniture to all kinds of businesses around town."

Cal called a week or so later and said, "Jack, I found something you might want to explore. I told one of my customers about you and they said they would be happy to interview you." He gave me the date and time to report to a company on the 18th floor of the Maryland National Bank building at 10 Light Street downtown, the tallest office building in the city at the time.

I stepped off the elevator on the 18th floor into rows and rows of guys plugging away behind their desks wearing white shirts and neckties—ties from my factory. I decided then and there that I didn't want to make ties anymore, I wanted to wear them!

The job was a clerical position in the office, which sounded great compared to sweeping floors and cleaning restrooms. The interviewer liked me, told me I could start in two weeks, and handed me his business card.

I glanced at the card, rode down the elevator, and ran home to pull out my English/German dictionary for some help in understanding what kind of company I just agreed to work for.

"American." That I got.

"Associated." *Assoziiert* in German, which means "related." Ok, but that didn't tell me much.

Then the word that stumped me. "Insurance." *Versicherung.* All I knew was that I unwittingly stumbled into an insurance company of some sort, a type of company I had never dealt with in my life.

When I gave notice to Miller's Tie Factory they offered me a position in sales, which came with a multi-state territory and a car. I was flattered, and thanked them, but explained that I wanted to run my own business someday and thought the insurance company offered a better training ground for me.

My first day at work at the American Associated Insurance Company

So, in the summer of 1951, exactly one year after I arrived in Baltimore, I began my first job in the insurance business.

When I showed up on my first day, the office manager, Mr. Stafford, showed me to my very own desk and plopped a stack of manuals in front of me. "Read these. They'll teach you about insurance," he said. I worked in the clerical division of the underwriting department. I wrote up all the information that the underwriters needed to decide whether or not to insure the businesses and individuals who applied for insurance.

I lived on a tight budget. I stopped at the Read's drug store at Howard and Lexington Streets every morning for the free Graham crackers they gave away with a cup of coffee. Breakfast of champions!

You never know who you're going to meet at the office. I became office friends with someone I admired—Maryland Governor Theodore McKeldin. He worked in an office on the 18th floor of my building and I spoke to him every day in the men's room.

I appreciated McKeldin for coming to Europe during the war to help persuade Allied Commander Dwight Eisenhower to run for president of the United States. I thought Eisenhower was one of the greatest people in the world for defeating Hitler. McKeldin introduced Eisenhower at the Republican Convention when Eisenhower won the nomination.

"I'm going to stay here"

I received a letter from my always-loving and over-protective older brother, Peter, letting me know that he had rented a place big enough for the both of us and even lined up a job for me. But living on my own in Baltimore I realized how much I valued making my own decisions for the first time in my life.

"I appreciate all you've done," I told Peter, "but I'm going to stay here." I think I hurt his feelings, but I was ready to fly out from under his wing. Things worked out fine for him. He married Elsa a few years later, and they had two children, Byron and Vivian.

"Restricted"

As the new guy at the American Associated Insurance Company, I drew the assignment of scouting out a place for the company picnic. "Look for something around the Chesapeake Bay," Mr. Stafford told me. He offered to lend me his car when I was ready to go out and look.

I took a couple of days to find a map—a paper map in those days—and ask a few friends for suggestions. Then I borrowed Mr. Stafford's car and hit the road. I was delighted to explore the Chesapeake Bay area, which I had never seen before. It brought back fond memories of fishing on the North Sea.

Several places where I stopped to check out displayed big signs on the wall that said, "RESTRICTED."

"What does 'restricted' mean?" I asked.

"No blacks, no Jews," they said.

You too, America?

People weren't hunted and killed like in Hitler's Germany, but it surprised and sickened me to discover antisemitism and racism in my new country. And as a practical matter, two Jews worked at American Associated Insurance—me, and Marty Baumgarten.

After checking a half-dozen locations I found the venue that I liked best, one of the biggest beaches on the Bay, outside of Annapolis. I decided not to let their "RESTRICTED" sign stop me so easily.

"But we only have one person," I said, counting myself as a Catholic.

I went back and forth a few times with them, arguing my case. "One person out of more than 70," I kept saying. Finally, they gave in. "Okay. Let's not talk about it anymore. Let's just do it. We'll make an exception."

The picnic was a hit. We swam, played tennis, and played softball. And Marty had a great time.

Kindred Spirits

Our landlady on North Calvert Street reached a point where she couldn't keep up the house anymore, and we had to move out. My friend Harold Hanson from the Sunday Evening Club was also looking for a new place so we roomed together in a brand-new apartment building at 1010 St. Paul Street.

Harold was one of the senior librarians at the Enoch Pratt Free Library, and we shared many interests. He was the only other person I had met who enjoyed going to museums, and there were so many around town—the Baltimore Museum of Art, the Walters Art Museum, the B&O Railroad Museum, the Edgar Allan Poe House—that we never ran out of fascinating exhibits to explore.

Harold also loved classical music and introduced me to the music room at the library where I basked for hours in the Mozart and Strauss masterpieces that I grew up with in Austria.

Kotja, my "half-brother" from Tante Irma's, kept his promise to follow me—not to the same city but at least to the same continent. He applied for emigration with the International Refugee Organization (IRO), which, like USCOM, helped homeless people relocate after the war. His aunt had already emigrated to Canada, which made Canada the destination where he would have the greatest likelihood of approval. He moved to Montreal in 1951 and, since he finished high school in Germany, enrolled at McGill University and majored in philosophy.

Kotja, me, and Harold on vacation in Quebec

When I told Harold about Kotja, he said, "We could take a vacation and drive up to see him if you'd like."

"I would love that, thank you!" I said.

We spent a few days with Kotja in Montreal, then the three of us went camping in Nova Scotia—where the mosquitos ate us alive—and sightseeing in Old Quebec City.

THE GOLDEN RULE

From the minute I stepped off the Greyhound bus it seemed like I always met the right person at the right time in Baltimore. When people heard my story they wanted to help me. I needed advice and guidance at times, and everything always worked out perfectly.

I believed in the Golden Rule and vowed that I would help others in the same way, and in November 1952 I got my chance when I heard from Tante Irma's son, Gernot. He had become a certified garden technician and designed gardens in Germany, Switzerland, and Sweden, but thought his professional opportunities were greater in America. He asked me to sponsor him for immigration and help him find landscaping work in Baltimore.

I agreed, but there was one complication. I thought I might be leaving Baltimore at any moment. I expected to be drafted into the United States Army and shipped out to Korea.

Chapter 11

DRAFTED

BALTIMORE, MARYLAND, USA
MORGANFIELD, KENTUCKY, USA
1952-1953

MY FRIENDS TOLD me that I could be drafted even though I wasn't a U.S. citizen, and I found out they were right when my brother Peter told me he had been drafted. At least they didn't send him into combat. His base was a houseboat in Trieste, Italy, and his duty was to transport incoming soldiers to their bases when they arrived at the train station.

I registered for the draft and prepared ahead of time in case my number came up. I asked Harold to sponsor Tante Irma's son Gernot for his immigration to America, and Harold didn't hesitate.

I also speeded up the process of earning my high school degree. I was afraid I wouldn't have time to take all the algebra and geometry and history and other requirements still left, so I applied to take the high school equivalency test so I would have my degree before going away to the army. That way I'd be ready to start college—tuition-free on the G.I. Bill—when I returned.

I crammed for weeks. It took a score of 75 to pass, and I eked out a 76.

I credit Herr Pille as much as my cramming for the point that lifted me over the top. By eighth grade, he had taught me much of the material that was on the exam. It's amazing, in comparison to American high schools, how much we learned in that little two-room village schoolhouse.

Basic Training

Life started to move fast. Gernot arrived in Baltimore in December 1952 and was pleased to discover that his garden design expertise exceeded those of his American counterparts. My draft number was called, and in January 1953, I reported to Fort Meade in Maryland for my army medical exams.

I didn't mind joining the army. It was my chance to pay the country back for letting me come. And Peter gave me some advice. "Learn how to type or somehow let them know you can do office work. Better to sit at a desk than in a foxhole."

One day at Fort Meade I was standing in formation and the sergeant asked, "Is there anyone here who can do some paperwork?"

Out of hundreds of us, three other guys and I stepped forward.

"Everyone back to the barracks except you four," the sergeant barked.

The sergeant walked up to us. "So you guys like paperwork? Well, I'll tell you what you're going to do. You see all the cigarette butts lying around here? Pick them up!"

"Thanks a lot for the advice, Peter," I told my brother the next time I talked to him.

I also applied for Officer Candidate School, which required an extra year of service, but education was a priority for me. I was accepted and waited to hear where they would send me. The sergeant called me into his office and gave me news I wasn't expecting.

"Wurfl, we're sorry, but you're not a citizen. You can't be an officer in the American Army if you're not a citizen of the United States. You'll report to basic training at Camp Breckenridge."

But there was a silver lining. When they saw on my army Form 40 that I spoke fluent German, they assigned me to the 101st Airborne Division, 1st Infantry, stationed in—I could hardly believe my ears—Germany. Out of 188 recruits, only two of us did not go to Korea—me, and a guy who spoke Norwegian whom they assigned to the military attaché in Oslo.

A couple of days later I took a troop train to Camp Breckenridge in Kentucky, and what a tragic introduction to the army that turned out to be. Our train accidentally struck a civilian's car and killed the two passengers.

The accident foreshadowed all the talk of killing over my four months of basic training.

"We're going to make killers out of you," they told us over and over.

"You're going to fight the Chinese or the Koreans over there. A lot of it is hand-to-hand combat, so you'd better learn to use your bayonet to stab and kill people."

This is not what I was looking for. This is not what I left Nazi Germany for.

Every morning, reveille sounded at 5 am. It wasn't unusual for a sergeant to storm in and holler, "Everybody up!"

We jumped out of our beds and snapped to attention, then the sergeant inspected our footlockers. God help you if he found something besides the clothes and gear that belonged in it.

Then the sergeant would yell, "Look at the floor." It rained a lot in Kentucky and if someone had tracked in the smallest speck of mud we'd hear, "Get your toothbrushes." We'd have to get down on our hands and knees and for the next hour scrub the floor with our toothbrushes.

At Camp Breckenridge for basic training

After the harassment, we exercised, ate breakfast, and marched to the drumbeats out to the fields for weapons training. Mostly we fired what the army called light-infantry weapons—pistols, M1 rifles, and machine guns.

Jumping out of planes for parachute training was the most dangerous aspect of my training. Landing in a tree could hurt. On windy days, if we didn't pull our chutes in quickly enough after landing, the wind would drag us across the countryside fields, and that also hurt.

In some ways, I was better prepared for basic training than most of the American guys. I grew up surrounded by the Gestapo and the SS and the police ordering what to do and where to go. I learned how to march and throw hand grenades and shoot weapons in Hitler Youth. Basic training felt like a continuation of my life in Germany.

We had a little downtime, and the base had a lounge where we could go in the evenings to relax and socialize. On occasion, bands would come in and local girls were invited for a dance, but usually, we were too tired for a social life.

AWOL

My friend Harold wrote to tell me he was getting married, and asked me to be his best man. What an honor! How could I say no? But there was no way my commanding officer would allow me to leave for a wedding.

So I didn't ask, and I left anyway.

On Harold's wedding day, I told some bull story to the security guards at the gate so they would let me off the base. I took a bus to the airport in Evansville, Indiana, boarded a flight to Baltimore, and then my worst nightmare came true. I sat down in an empty row and watched the rest of the passengers board. I broke into a sweat when the Commanding General and Assistant Commanding General of the 101st Airborne walked down the aisle toward me.

Busted and nowhere to hide!

Then they sat down next to me!

I was shaking in my boots the whole flight but they never asked where I was going or what I was doing off base. So lucky!

Harold's wedding was beautiful, and I flew right back to the base and used the same excuse to get past the guards, no questions asked.

Gott sei Dank! (Thank God!)

"A TREMENDOUS MIXTURE"

The grand finale of my four months of basic training was the infiltration course, a combat-simulation exercise. They took us to a field of foot-deep mud lined with barbed wire. As we crawled through the mud they shot 30-caliber machine guns over our heads to make sure we stayed low and crawled with the proper technique.

The biggest non-military lesson I learned in basic training was how to get along with people from a tremendous mix of races, ethnicities, and life backgrounds. Living with 60 guys in barracks lined with bunk beds and training 24/7 to go into combat with them, I discovered that our differences didn't matter.

The diversity gave me the privilege of meeting people I probably wouldn't have in any other setting—like my mate who slept in the bunk below me. He couldn't read or write and asked me to read his wife's letters to him. Then he would dictate to me a letter I would write back to her.

After basic training, the army gave us nine days of leave before our deployments. I went home to say goodbye to Harold and his new bride and my other friends, then reported to Camp Kilmer in New Jersey to begin my tour of duty.

Chapter 12

TOUR OF DUTY

WURZBURG, GERMANY, 1953-1954

FROM CAMP KILMER, the army loaded me on a train to New York, then stuffed me with thousands of other soldiers on a tiny troop ship to Germany. I was lucky to find a spot to sit down on the deck, and we slept in hammocks stacked four and five on top of each other. We lived like sardines for twelve days.

One of my mates who slept near me had a chess set, and we played every day to pass the time.

After docking in Germany I took a train to Wurzburg, about 300 miles from Dangast, and reported to the headquarters of the 1st Infantry Division, a division of about 20,000 soldiers.

We were lucky to find a place to sit on the troop ship to Germany

The former German Army barracks I stayed in were pretty nice. We bunked four to a room, and I got along fine with my roommates. I became friends with a few guys around the barracks: Truman Kennedy, from Cleveland; Tex, from Texas; Jeff, from Idaho, and a teacher from Chicago whose name escapes me.

CLASSIFICATION AND ASSIGNMENT

I worked in the Classification and Assignment unit. About 200 American replacement soldiers arrived at the Wurzburg railroad station every month. My job was to drive a Jeep to the station and pick up the box of Form 20s—the personal profiles of all the new arrivals. Over the next couple of days, I read each soldier's background and assigned each of them a duty.

At work on classification and assignment duty

But I didn't make the assignments the way my sergeant wanted me to. He had a chip on his shoulder against college students and graduates and wanted them digging holes or out on maneuvers all the time. But he drank beer all day and wasn't always in the office or aware of the soldiers' backgrounds, so I assigned everyone according to where we could best use their education and experience.

I loved the job because I had responsibilities that helped people and made the army work more effectively.

My duties also included compiling the "morning reports." Every morning each platoon lined up for roll call, and the troop counts were recorded on a report. Once a month I had to consolidate the daily reports and deliver them to an army base 100 miles away near Frankfurt, Germany. The reports were considered top secret so they shackled a briefcase to my wrist and flew me to Frankfurt by helicopter.

In addition to assigning duties and compiling the morning reports, the American, French, and British colonels and generals called on me whenever they needed something translated from or into German. They called me quite often because they were training the *Deutsche Volkspolizei* (German People's Police), the name for the new German Army.

I'd go out on maneuvers with the People's Police and the international forces for weeks at a time. I traveled all over Germany with them—once in the middle of winter into the woods, where we had to shovel snow to clear spaces for our tents. I met some of the best and brightest officers in the world and learned everything about modern military strategy as I translated their commands and instructions.

I worked on translations for happier occasions also. I translated marriage papers for an American soldier and his German bride. On weekends when I was out with the guys and meeting German girls, I didn't always let on to the girls that I spoke German. That gave me a tremendous advantage when the girls spoke among themselves in German about which girl liked which of us guys, thinking we didn't know what they were saying. I knew where we all stood and passed along the intel to my buddies.

When I was out on maneuvers translating, I still had to keep up with my classification and assignment duties. I'd set up a table and typewriter in a tent and work on the new arrival assignments between translation sessions.

Fish Stories

Life on the base wasn't all work and no play. I played a set or two of tennis just about every day, and worked my way into fishing trips with my colonel.

Colonel Miller, an officer of the 1st Infantry Division, was a fanatic trout fisherman. He figured that since I grew up in Germany I would be the best person to scout fishing locations for him.

Once a month or so he'd call me on the phone and say, "Wurfl, come up to my office for a minute. I have something to discuss with you."

I found time for tennis almost every day

TOUR OF DUTY

I'd walk into his office and he'd stand in front of his huge map of Germany on the wall and point to a stream or river. "I'd like to find some good fishing in this area for next weekend. I've invited another colonel and a general to go with me.

"I want you to take my car and find out where we can fish in that area. Contact the property owners and get permission from them. And let the German police know we're coming. And find a hotel where we can stay and can cook the trout for us."

I'd hop in his Pontiac and drive around to make all the arrangements.

Colonel Miller and his fishing buddies always asked me to go with them on their trip in case they needed an interpreter, even though it broke the army rule against enlisted men like me mingling with officers like them. "Don't tell anyone that we're taking you with us," they always warned me.

I joined them on a dozen or more outings, and Colonel Miller always brought an extra rod for me. I fished alongside him and the other army brass, and no one ever found out. We ate a lot of trout, which I liked—but not nearly as much as I liked a smoked eel.

One day Colonel Miller called me into his office for a different kind of fishing expedition. He had so much success catching trout with his German-made lure that he wanted to find the manufacturer and sign a deal as their exclusive distributor in the United States after he retired from the army.

As his translator, I found and contacted the manufacturer and helped Colonel Miller negotiate a deal that set him up for a future business. We became good friends through our shared love of fishing.

Familiar Faces

Part of my deployment in Wurzburg overlapped with Peter's tour of duty in Italy. We saw each other a few times when we could take leave.

I also took leave a few times to make the 300-mile train ride to visit Tante Irma in Dangast. We hugged, laughed, and loved seeing each other. It took her a while to get used to seeing her adopted son dressed in a U.S. Army uniform—the uniform of the country that bombed her beloved homeland.

In the summer of 1953, she asked if I could come and do her a favor. Now 61 years old, she had decided to leave Germany and join her son Gernot to work at

Visiting Tante Irma in Dangast

the Valley Mart garden center in Baltimore. Waltraud and her husband, Willy, had moved back to Irmenfried, and Waltraud had taken over the management of the camp.

"Can you take me to the ship in Bremerhaven to make sure I get off okay?" she asked.

I was happy to help Tante Irma get to Baltimore, though I didn't expect her to leave so soon. A few months later, she and Gernot moved to Colorado Springs where Gernot founded his own landscape architecture business. I wish we could have lived in the same city, but I was happy for her because, after 30 years of interruptions, her tenacity and drive paid off and she could work in her chosen profession.

A Good Citizen

Our division did its best to be a good neighbor in the Wurzburg community. In 1953 we sponsored Christmas dinners and luncheons for the children at the Wurzburg Institute for the Blind, and gave each child a Christmas present. Our

Above: Christmas dinner at the Wurzburg Institute for the Blind

Below: My first day as a U.S. citizen!

division newspaper, *The American Traveler*, wrote a story about the event and happened to come to my table for pictures!

Around that same holiday season, the United States enacted a new citizenship policy. Permanent residents who had lived in the U.S. for at least a year and served at least 90 days in the military could become U.S. citizens.

I applied immediately since the normal waiting time was five years and I could become a citizen a year sooner. In March 1954, at age 21, I swore my oath of allegiance to the United States of America at a ceremony in Frankfurt, Germany.

Remembering D-Day

Back at the base in Wurzburg, I was walking from my barracks to my office one day when someone stopped me.

"The company commander wants to see you," he said.

When I reported to his office he said, "Wurfl, I've been watching you walk back and forth from the headquarters building and you have a good, straight walk. You don't hunch over. I'd like you to be in the division's color guard."

The color guard consists of four soldiers. Two corporais on the outside carry rifles—one of those would be my position. Two sergeants on the inside carry flags—the division flag and the American flag. To be selected for the color guard was an honor, and also came with certain privileges, including more liberty to leave the base without a pass and opportunities to travel around Europe marching in parades and other special military events.

The only downside was the early-morning and late-night practices.

"It will be an honor, sir," I said.

In June 1954 my captain notified me that the color guard would be reporting to Normandy, France.

"What is the occasion in Normandy?" I asked.

He explained that the 1st Infantry Division was one of the first to storm Omaha Beach on D-Day, so we were invited to march in the 10th-anniversary celebration of the invasion.

Every country and every unit that participated in the invasion sent its honor guard and color guard. The Americans, the British with their fancy tunics and tall caps, the Norwegians, the Canadians, and the French reunited for two

*Marching past the Allied graveyard at Normandy on the
10th anniversary of D-Day. I'm carrying the rifle on the far left.*

weeks of ceremonies, celebrations, and parades.

The occasion was so important that the army "promoted" me and the other rifleman to add prestige to our color guard. We were both only corporals, but they gave us uniforms with sergeant stripes to wear in the parades. I got a kick out of senior officers from every country saluting me and offering a "Good afternoon, sergeant" as they passed me.

How amazing. On D-Day, I had huddled around the radio in Dangast, Germany, listening to the BBC news of the invasion and hoping that it meant the war would soon end. Ten years later I wore a U.S. Army uniform and marched amidst the beaches and graveyards and monuments.

I paraded in front of President Eisenhower, British Prime Minister Winston Churchill, and French President Charles de Gaulle. One morning at sunrise I stood on Utah Beach on the edge of the English Channel while a bugler blew taps at General Theodore Roosevelt Jr.'s gravesite.

What a tremendous privilege to serve there. And to think, I could have been lying in the woods in Korea.

In Search of My Father

Wurzburg is less than 300 miles from Austria, and while I was stationed there I couldn't help but think about the country of my birth and my father. Eight years after the war I still had no idea what had happened to him. I took leave and bought a train ticket to Linz, where my father grew up. I'd check around the town, and visit the Mauthausen concentration camp where he was imprisoned, to try to find out something, anything.

At my hotel in Linz, I got to thinking, *I wonder if there are any Wurfls left in Linz*. I opened the phone book and found a Franz Wurfl! My uncle! One of my father's brothers who left Austria in 1938! I dialed the number.

"What are you doing in Linz?" Uncle Franz asked. I explained that I was in the U.S. Army on leave from my post in Germany.

"What are you doing in the U.S. Army?"

"Let's meet and I'll tell you everything that's happened." Then I asked him, "What are you doing in Linz?"

"I'm searching for my wife," he said. She was a Jewish native of France who left Ecuador to visit her relatives in France just before the war and "disappeared." Uncle Franz was searching all the concentration camps in Europe looking for information about her.

We spent several days catching up on each other's lives. One day while we were walking down the street, Uncle Franz stopped and said, "Hey, look! It's Hans!"

"Who's Hans?" I asked.

"One of your father's best friends."

"Oh my God," I said, "can we meet him?"

"Of course, we have to meet him," he said, and called Hans over to us.

"Hans, I want you to meet someone. Guess who this American soldier is," Uncle Franz said.

Hans looked at me, tilted his head, and shrugged. "Sorry, I have no idea."

"This is Jochen Wurfl, Karl's son!"

Hans reached back, pulled out his billfold, and showed me an old picture of my parents, Peter, and me. The three of us teared up. That was one of the most amazing things that ever happened to me—meeting a total stranger who had been carrying around a picture of my family for fifteen years.

"Your parents were my best friends," he said.

Over the week I spent with Uncle Franz, he told me that during his search for his wife, he had also asked around about my father. He found out that the Americans liberated him from Mauthausen, but he contracted tuberculosis there and had withered to only 80 pounds by the time he was released.

The U.S. Army doctors asked a farming family near Linz, named Luger, to take care of him, thinking it would be a healthy environment for recovery. "Would you like to meet the Lugers?" Uncle Franz asked.

"Of course!" I said. "I want to thank them for trying to save my father."

The Lugers were very, very lovely people. They told me how hard my father tried to get better. How careful he was not to eat too much too soon—after practically starving for years, too much food would have killed him. Three doctors treated him: Dr. Reichel, a lung specialist, a doctor named Monauni, and the supervising doctor, a woman named Malissa. A Polish orderly named Ladi also helped take care of him.

But tuberculosis had already destroyed both of his lungs and was spreading throughout his body. He died after about two months. What a sad, sad irony that a man who survived seven war years in concentration camps, escaped twice, and was liberated, died so shortly after tasting freedom again.

I wanted to make sure I remembered everything the Lugers told me, so I pulled the only piece of paper I had out of my pocket—a street map of Berlin that the Hotel Stephanie had given me—and jotted notes.

The only detail the Lugers didn't know was where the town officials buried my father's body.

Uncle Franz told me that he looked for my father's grave but never found it. Over the next several days I looked in every graveyard in the area but never found him. I looked for the doctors who treated him but none of them were still in Linz. But at least I knew where and how my father died. Uncle Franz never found out anything about what happened to his wife.

My map from 1954 is torn and tattered, but my notes about my father's doctors and other information the Luger family provided are crystal clear

"Our differences didn't matter"

My two-year commitment to the army ended in December 1954. I loved my job and made wonderful friends, but I couldn't see myself making a career in the army and did not re-enlist. I received an honorable discharge as a corporal.

I took home lifelong lessons that I couldn't have learned anywhere else but in the army. I grew up in Germany under an oppressive dictatorship where unless you were a blond-haired, blue-eyed Aryan person, you didn't count. I always knew in my heart that was wrong, but in the army, I experienced the truth day in and day out. I ate at the same tables, worked and trained in the same uniform, and slept in the same rows of cots with people of every race and religion, college-educated and illiterate, American-born and immigrants.

My experience taught me to understand and appreciate all people, their customs, and their way of thinking. I learned that I needed to find out what they're all about, and respect them for who they are. I got along with so many different kinds of people because I discovered that our differences didn't matter.

Chapter 13

NEW BEGINNINGS

BALTIMORE, MARYLAND, USA, 1955

THE ARMY STUFFED me and 5,000 other soldiers on a troop ship back to New York. A hurricane whipped up in the Atlantic, and the thirty-foot waves rocked the ship so violently that I had to tie myself to the rail to keep from falling overboard. I stayed up on the top deck because the icy wind and rain were more tolerable than the stench from all the seasick, vomiting soldiers down below.

I was just happy to be on my way back to the United States. Once you've lived anywhere else, you realize there's no country like the United States, where there's democracy, and the freedom to do whatever you want. I looked forward to reuniting with my friends and getting back to my job at the American Associated Insurance Company. I dreamed of building my own business someday.

I returned to Baltimore at age 22 in December 1954. American Associated Insurance hired me back, and I enrolled at the University of Baltimore (UB), where I planned to take every insurance course they offered. The government paid my tuition through the G.I. Bill.

One of the first friends that I called was Ben Paredes, the guy I met in my high school classes at City High School and who worked at the El Salvador consulate. "Great to have you back!" he said. "We're throwing a New Year's Eve party and all the people from the South American embassies will be there. I'd like you to come."

Zonia Nusen, Miss El Salvador

"Thanks, I'd love to," I said. "Who knows, maybe I'll meet a nice girl!"

"Maybe you will," Ben said. "The party's at the Pan American Club on Mount Royal Avenue. See you there!"

It was a big, formal party, and very Latino. I learned how to dance the mambo, and Ben introduced me to a girl he knew from the El Salvador consulate named Zonia. She had worked at the El Salvador embassy in Washington but now managed the consulate in Baltimore. She spoke little English and I knew about 50 Spanish words, but I liked her right away. Ben translated for us and we hit it off.

I told her about growing up in Germany and coming to America. Ben casually mentioned that Zonia was a former Miss El Salvador and competed in the Miss Universe pageant, and that her uncle had been the President of El Salvador in the 1930s and 1940s.

Are you kidding me?

As we were leaving the party I asked her if she would go out with me on a date.

"Yes, give me a call," she said.

Zonia lived in Baltimore near the YWCA on Franklin Street at an apartment house for Catholic women called the Cadoa. When I picked her up for our date, the house mother—not a nun but the closest thing to one—answered the door, told me to sit down in a little waiting room, and walked upstairs to tell Zonia I was there. Before we left, the lady instructed us to "try to be back before midnight."

NEW BEGINNINGS

We went out for dinner and a movie and enjoyed another nice time together. I dropped her off before curfew, and she agreed to go out with me again.

Used Car, New Job, New School

Since it looked like I would be dating regularly, I figured I would make a better impression on Zonia and any other girls if I owned a car and didn't have to rely on borrowing one or taking public transportation. I found a 1947 Chevrolet for $300 and applied for a loan at the bank, but they turned me down.

One day I happened to mention my predicament to an agent who sent his business to American Associated Insurance. "I can help you," he said. "I have contacts at the Manchester Bank in Carroll County."

He talked to his contacts and Manchester Bank lent me the $300, which took me two years to pay back. My eight-year-old Chevy wasn't the fancy Studebaker or Packard I dreamed about on my first day in New York, but I had something to drive on a date, and that was the important thing.

After six months of working at American Associated Insurance and studying insurance at the University of Baltimore, I realized how to make the big money in the insurance industry. It wasn't by sitting behind a desk on the underwriting side where I worked, but by selling insurance on the agency side. After that epiphany, I began searching for a new job at an agency.

I interviewed at all the bigger agencies in town and they all said, "Yes, you can start tomorrow." But when I told them that I wanted all the accounts I brought in to be mine, even if I left the company, they balked. "We'll pay you a commission, but if you ever leave, the business belongs to the agency, not to you."

"I'll get back to you," I told them.

I expanded my search to smaller agencies and found one, Keiser & Keiser on Commerce Street near City Hall, that agreed to let me own my accounts. I had found what I was looking for, and I accepted their offer.

I made my first sale to my new roommate, Rick Amador. We lived in an apartment on Canterbury Road behind Homewood Field near Johns Hopkins University and I insured his beat-up old Ford which was missing the passenger-side door.

I couldn't make a living off of beat-up cars so I told my boss, Klaus Buchdal, that I wanted to call on a successful, Jewish-owned restaurant chain with thirteen locations called the White Coffee Pot.

"No, they're too big for us. They want to deal with a big agency," he said.

"Well, I think I can get them," I said. I had a different way of thinking and a different approach than the owners of the agency. I lived in the land of opportunity and I would never say that an account was too big.

I called the White Coffee Pot and they gave me an appointment. I talked to them about their insurance and built a relationship with them over several months. I never gave up, and finally closed what became Keiser & Keiser's largest account, with a premium of $40,000 a year.

Klaus Buchdal of Keiser & Keiser

They told me it couldn't be done, but I proved that we could win those kinds of accounts. Closing White Coffee Pot gave me the confidence that I could do anything.

Now even more motivated to pursue a career in insurance, I began taking additional insurance courses at Loyola College.

WEDDING BELLS

Zonia and I started seeing each other just about every day, going out to movies, dances, embassy parties, and dinner parties with friends in Baltimore and Washington. We enjoyed long walks along Loch Raven Reservoir—which at that time people considered out in the wilderness—and shopping. Zonia loved the downtown department stores on Howard Street—Hecht's, Hochschild Kohn, Hutzler's, and the May Company.

It didn't take Zonia long to realize that shopping was not my thing. "How come you always wear the same shoes?" she asked me one day.

I was embarrassed but told her the truth. "They're the only shoes I have."

Language was never a barrier between us. We thought speaking different languages was fun. It wasn't a spoken language, but the language of feelings that kept us wanting to be together.

Zonia's family history fascinated me. Her father, Edmundo Nusen, was born and raised in Paris. As a young man, he traveled to El Salvador and met a girl named Blanca. They fell in love, got married, and raised Zonia and her four siblings in El Salvador.

Zonia was born a year after her uncle, General Maximiliano Hernández Martínez, became the Acting President of El Salvador in 1931. He held that title until 1935 when he was chosen as the 30th President of El Salvador, and held office until 1944.

He accomplished so much good for the country—built new roads, new schools, and hospitals, expanded voting rights to women for the first time, and enacted social security programs—that El Salvador honored him with a commemorative postage stamp that is still used today. Yet at the same time, he ruled with an iron fist to stave off his political enemies, the way most Latin American presidents ran their governments then.

Zonia's family worked in government jobs while her uncle was President, and Zonia lived with her uncle and aunt in the presidential residence—the El Salvador White House, as they called it. Zonia was Uncle Maximiliano's favorite little girl, and as she grew up he spoiled her with nice clothes, high-society events, and country club memberships.

But somehow she fell in love with me, a guy who owned one pair of shoes. After dating for about a year, I asked her to marry me. "Yes," she said, "I love you and want to marry you. And I'd like to live in the United States."

After Zonia said "yes," I wrote to her parents in El Salvador to introduce myself and tell them I wanted to marry their daughter. They wrote back and said, "If she loves you, and wants to marry you, you have our permission." We were both 23 years old when we got engaged.

Not long after our engagement, Zonia's Uncle Maximiliano, who had been out of office for ten years at that point, wrote to say he was coming to Baltimore for medical tests at Johns Hopkins Hospital. But why Hopkins, and why now? I think he wanted to check out the guy who wanted to marry his favorite niece.

I chauffeured him around Baltimore for a week. I thought he was a wonderful man, and he tacitly gave Zonia and me his blessing for marriage.

Zonia was a devout Catholic with a strong faith in God and wanted to be married in the Catholic church. I had been baptized Catholic so that was fine with me, even though I wasn't raised to practice Catholicism, Judaism, or any religion. But since I hadn't received the Catholic sacraments of holy communion or confirmation, there were a few stipulations and conditions I had to agree to before we could be married in the Church. I was happy to go along with all of them.

First, the Church asked me to meet with a priest for ten classes on Catholicism. I met with Father Madagar at the Basilica on Cathedral Street. Zonia attended church there because it was close to the Cadoa where she lived. The Basilica was well known as the first Roman Catholic cathedral built in the United States, but I remembered it as the church where Mr. Libertini found a place for Peter and me to sleep our first night in Baltimore.

I enjoyed my conversations with Father Madagar. They were very educational for me, and Father was such a fantastic person that I grew to love him.

I also agreed that if we had children, they would be raised Catholic and I would attend Mass with the family—not necessarily every week, but often. Lastly, because I had not received all the Catholic sacraments, we could get married in the

Our wedding day, April 21, 1956

NEW BEGINNINGS

church, but not in the sanctuary. The ceremony had to take place in the front section of the church.

Zonia and I were married at the Basilica on April 21, 1956. Father Madagar performed the ceremony. About fifteen guests attended, including Zonia's mother, Blanca, and my brother, Peter, who spotted me $50 to pay for the church. After the ceremony, we all enjoyed dinner at the Chesapeake Restaurant on Charles Street. The Chesapeake was one of the classiest restaurants in town and the dinner cost us plenty—around $10 per person.

For our honeymoon, we stayed one night at the Belvedere Hotel downtown. We spent half of the evening watching highlights on television of quite a different style of wedding—the "wedding of the century" of Prince Rainier of Monaco and the American actress Grace Kelly. Their ceremonies and receptions, part of which took place in a palace and a cathedral with 700 guests, spanned two days.

Our palace was a tiny apartment on the bottom floor of a house on Rexmere Road behind the old Memorial Stadium on 33rd Street. When we moved in I was surprised that it didn't have a refrigerator, so I had to put out $50 for a used one, which left us with almost no money to our name.

Chapter 14

SOMEONE SPECIAL

BALTIMORE, MARYLAND, USA, 1956-1960

BLANCA ALSO SURPRISED us with her announcement that she wanted to stay in Baltimore for "a couple of weeks" with us in our apartment. Now, don't get me wrong. I loved Blanca. She was a wonderful woman, we got along great. She slept in the living room, but to use the bathroom or fix something in the kitchen, Blanca had to walk through our bedroom. When that could happen any time day or night, it created some embarrassing moments.

Blanca's "couple of weeks" stretched into four months, which made for more embarrassing moments, and turned out to be very expensive for me.

Before she left at the end of the summer of 1956, Blanca asked Zonia to take her shopping at the stores on Howard Street. Blanca charged thousands and thousands of dollars' worth of clothes on Zonia's credit card. "You can't get clothes like these in El Salvador," she said to me when they got home. "I'm going to open a store and sell them," she explained as she stuffed the clothes into duffel bags. "Then I'll pay you back."

Thirty days later, the bill arrived but not a penny from Blanca. Flustered and deep in debt, the only way out I could think of was to ask my boss for a loan.

"Why? What's going on?" Mr. Buchdal asked, and I explained what had happened. Mr. Buchdal didn't give me a loan; he gave me a lesson in budgeting and negotiating.

He said, "I want you to write down how much money you and your wife make each month, and how much you need for rent, food, and other necessities—only the necessities. Then you'll know how much you have left to pay off the stores.

"Go see the credit manager at Hutzler's and the Hecht Company and the May Company and explain what happened. Show them your budget and tell them how much you can pay back each month, and ask them not to charge you any interest."

Terrific advice. Every credit manager understood my predicament and said, "Okay, as long as you pay something every month, we won't charge any interest, however long it takes."

Phew!

It took Blanca only a few hours to rack up those bills; it took Zonia and me several years to pay them off.

Thanks, But No Thanks

The credit card debt made me hustle even harder at work. I landed several new accounts, which increased both my income and my stature at Keiser & Keiser. I was so happy with my situation at the agency that I declined a couple of unsolicited job offers.

One day at the office I got a call from the front desk on the first floor of the building. "There's a Colonel Miller here to see you."

Oh my gosh!

"So great to see you!" I said. Colonel Miller told me that he had retired from the army, moved to Florida, and, just as planned, had opened a distributorship for the German fishing-lure manufacturer. Then he offered me a job as the sales representative for the Maryland-DC-Virginia area.

Driving around selling fishing lures to fishing-tackle stores did not appeal to me at all. "Thank you," I said, "but I'm sorry, I'm going to stay in the insurance business."

A while later, Peter and I both received a letter from an uncle through marriage, Hans Levore, in Johannesburg, South Africa. He owned a factory that processed cheeses and sausages and all kinds of foods, and offered both of us jobs.

Peter had divorced Elsa, and in 1960, married Anita, our first cousin—which was legal and genetically safe. Peter said the job was "too good to pass up," when we talked about it on the phone. "It's a huge business. He's a multi-millionaire. We're his nephews so I'm sure we'll do well."

I said, "But Peter, we're in the land of paradise. I'm so happy to be here. You can go, but I'm not leaving America." I saw a future for myself in this country with its true freedom and democracy. I didn't want to leave for a government in the early stages of enforcing *apartheid* (racial separation) and a job with an uncle I didn't even know.

Peter left New York for South Africa, and I was sad to think that I would rarely ever see him. I liked living independently from him, but it would have been nice to live on the same continent.

LITTLE ODETTE

There are certain moments in life that you don't forget. In the summer of 1957, we had enough money for Zonia to visit her family in El Salvador for two months. I stayed home because I couldn't leave work for that long.

The day Zonia returned and I picked her up at the airport was one of the happiest days of my life.

In those days at Friendship Airport, which is now called the Baltimore-Washington International Thurgood Marshall Airport, arriving passengers walked down the steps of the plane and across the tarmac into the terminal.

I'll never forget the moment I saw Zonia coming down the steps of the airplane. From inside the terminal looking out the window, I spotted her—tanned, beautiful, smiling—and showing a baby bump! I don't think I ever loved her any more than at that instant, one of the most indelible moments of pure happiness in my life.

Zonia was due just before Christmas, which made decorating and trimming a little tree for the baby so much fun. She went into labor at Johns Hopkins Hospital on December 18, 1957. Fathers were not allowed in the delivery room then, so I sat in a waiting room and wondered whether I would have a son or a daughter. I sat and waited some more. And sat and waited some more. It seemed like the baby didn't want to come out.

Zonia was in labor for three days. I never left the hospital.

At long last, on December 20, a nurse burst into the waiting room and smiled at me.

"It's a girl!"

I sprang up from my chair and, through a glass window, adored my little daughter. The next day they let me hold her. Glorious!

The reason Zonia labored for so long was that the doctor had to resort to forceps to pull the baby out of the womb. In my eyes, she rated a 10 on the beauty scale, but her head looked a little stretched out. When I asked the doctor about it later, all he said was, "It was a difficult delivery."

Zonia and I both loved the French name Odette, which was Zonia's younger sister's name, and chose it for our daughter. Middle names were a new concept for me because no one in Austria or Germany, including me, has a middle name. For Odette, we agreed on Margaret, after my mother.

We brought Odette home on Christmas Eve, and she made that Christmas one of our happiest ever. We invited Ben Paredes, Rick Amador, and other friends over to show her off. I also showed off the skills I had learned at the new-parent classes that Zonia and I took at the Red Cross. I bathed Odette and fixed her formula every day.

BIG ODETTE

The following summer, when Odette was about six months old, Blanca asked us if Zonia's sister—the other Odette, eleven years old—could visit us for a couple of weeks. "Of course," we said. We'd be crowded in the apartment, but Zonia loved her younger sister and it would be nice to have "Big Odette" to help us with "Little Odette."

Big Odette loved living in America with us, and we were happy to have her. As the new school year approached we talked with her and Blanca about how much better the schools were in the U.S., and all of us liked the idea of Big Odette extending her stay and going to school in Baltimore. So once again, Blanca's weeks turned into months.

By the time school ended and the summer of 1959 rolled around, Zonia and I thought of Big Odette, now a teenager, as another daughter. We thought, why should she go back to El Salvador now? She'll have better schools and a better future in the U.S. She stayed in school in Baltimore, and in December celebrated Little Odette's second birthday with us.

"You have to tackle your problems in life"

When Zonia and I were around other two-year-olds, we noticed that Little Odette seemed behind most of them in her speech, her ability to follow directions, and even her walking. And one day she scared us when she passed out for no apparent reason. She regained consciousness quickly, but we wasted no time scheduling an appointment at Johns Hopkins.

They called her fainting a seizure. She had several more episodes, though none were serious. After a series of tests, the doctors diagnosed her with a disorder of the electrical signals in her brain. "She might outgrow it as a teenager," they said.

Could the forceps squeezing Little Odette's head at her birth be the cause? I've always thought so.

The doctors treated it with medication, and I took Little Odette to Hopkins every few months for them to measure the electrical capacity in her brain. We were thankful that the seizures subsided and Little Odette's functioning improved, but we feared that she would always have challenges.

Raising a special-needs child was a challenge for Zonia and me, but nothing could change the joy she brought to our lives and how much we loved her. We adjusted our lives to do whatever we had to for her. For me, that included withdrawing from college. I had completed the equivalent of two or three years of classes, but now I had other priorities.

You have to tackle your problems in life. You don't turn them over to someone else, and you don't give up.

Chapter 15

NEW HOUSE, NEW BABIES

LUTHERVILLE, MARYLAND, USA, 1961-1969

ZONIA AND I always thought that we would have multiple children, and in the spring of 1961, Zonia told me she was pregnant again. We were both 28 years old and ecstatic! We were also busting at the seams in our apartment so we started looking for a house.

New housing construction boomed in suburban Baltimore County around the Loch Raven Reservoir where we liked to take walks. We looked in the Towson, Lutherville, and Timonium areas and fell in love with a split-level house at 1212 Longford Road in Lutherville. The neighborhood teemed with young families with children and was two blocks from Hampton Elementary School.

But how could I afford a $17,500 house with a $165 monthly mortgage payment? Zonia had stopped working at the consulate after Little Odette's birth so we were living on only my income. I figured I would just have to sell more insurance or get a second job to make it work, and we bought it.

Morning sickness plagued Zonia so severely that she spent most of the nine months in bed. The day we moved into our new house, I set up our bedroom first so she could lie down while I moved in everything else. Except for spending a couple of weeks at the hospital because she couldn't keep any food down, she rarely left the house. Big Odette, then a tenth-grader at Dulaney High School, was a huge help. She and I took care of Zonia, four-year-old Little Odette, and all the cooking, cleaning, shopping, and yardwork.

Our next-door neighbors moved in around the same time so we saw each other coming and going quite often. The husband, Bill, and I became friendly, and one day while we were chatting he lowered his voice as if he wanted to tell me a secret. "I have to ask you a question," he said. "Your wife . . . did you marry a child bride?"

He thought Big Odette was my wife! He must have been wondering about it for a while before he got up the nerve to ask. I had to laugh.

Zonia went into labor on January 11, 1962, at Sinai Hospital. Zonia's father, Edmundo, came from El Salvador a few days before so he could wait at the hospital with me. We braced ourselves for another marathon delivery, but the nurse surprised us with how quickly she came out with the news.

"Congratulations! You have another girl!"

"Darn it. I wanted a boy," Edmundo said.

"Not me! I wanted another girl!" I said. "I love little girls!"

We named her Dana Jenine.

Zonia and I found it much easier to take care of our second baby compared with our first because this time we knew exactly what to do. Zonia took over bathing and formula-making duties. We already had the crib, high chair, toys, clothes and other supplies we needed. We signed up for a diaper service and the truck came once a week to bring clean diapers and take away the soiled ones. Big Odette loved nothing better than taking care of her little live doll, and Dana bonded with her almost as strongly as with Zonia.

Family Life

The kids grew up in a delightful, eclectic mix of El Salvadoran, Austrian, German, and American customs and traditions.

Zonia's English improved gradually over the years, and the girls spoke both English and Spanish at home. Zonia prepared a lot of Spanish meals. Paella was her specialty, a dish made with rice, saffron, green beans, lima beans, chicken, and shrimp. No one ever cooked it better than she did. She'd shop all day for the perfect ingredients and then spend two days cooking.

We also looked forward to her *frijoles* (refried beans), chicken in tomato sauce, tamales, and tortillas.

I introduced the family to Tante Irma's Christmas traditions, and we've kept them going to this day. I don't seal off a Christmas Room and bake for three days, but I do find stores that import cookies and candies from Germany and Austria. Marzipan, a candy made with sugar, honey, and almond paste, is still a family favorite. I fill Christmas plates with treats for everyone.

I decorate the tree—with electric lights, not burning candles—with Zonia's nativity scene under it. On Christmas Eve, I play records with traditional German Christmas songs like *Stille Nacht* (Silent Night), *O Tannenbaum* (O Christmas Tree), and *Leise rieselt der Schnee* (Softly Falls the Snow), and the children open their gifts.

Easter was more Americanized. Zonia would fix a big breakfast and I'd set up an Easter egg hunt.

I kept my promise to Father Madagar and attended Catholic Mass with the family—always on Christmas and Easter, and many Sundays throughout the year. The girls also attended CCD classes twice a week, the Catholic religious education program for children in public schools. Zonia continued to find strength from her faith, but neither she nor Father Madagar pressured me to fully convert to Catholicism.

I've always believed in God and the Almighty somewhere, somehow. But my mother and grandparents were not religious Jews, and Tante Irma's family were atheists, so I never had the privilege of growing up in the practice of any religion.

I was always happy when I met someone who told me about their faith in God, whether they were Jewish, Catholic, Muslim, or any religion. The basic commandments to do the right things, like the Golden Rule, are very similar.

Climbing the Ladder

As Little Odette approached kindergarten age in 1963, her doctors suggested a special-needs school because she was slower in her thinking and learning. I was 31 years old and working my way up the ladder at Keiser & Keiser so I could afford the tuition at a Catholic special-needs school in Roland Park and hire a bus company to pick her up and take her home every day.

My income grew both from selling more and taking on more responsibilities of managing the agency. "You're doing a better job than we have been doing," the owners, Norman Keiser and Klaus Buchdal, told me. They knew only one way to run the business—the same way Norman's grandfather had run it more than 50 years before. They had no imagination and no boldness to take risks.

Eventually, I managed the entire company. Norman and Klaus allowed me to make certain changes but drew a line at two ideas that were important to me. "We've done very well together," I told them. "You like me and I like you, but I'd like to have an ownership stake in the agency besides my own clients."

If they had offered me 5% of the stock, I would have been happy. But Norman spoke up and said, "Jack, we think the world of you. You're doing a great job and we need you here, but we are not going to give any part of the business away. It's a family business. I have a son in college who's going to come in and eventually take over."

I also approached Norman and Klaus with an innovative strategy for acquiring new business that I was 100% certain would bring in a windfall. "There are 14,000 trade associations in the country," I said. "Relationships are important for selling insurance, so I can visit the association offices in Washington or state capitals and go to their annual meetings. That way I'll know how to develop an insurance program for their member companies.

"Their members will like it because they can get better insurance, and the associations will like it because it will help them attract more members."

"No need to do all that," Norman said. "It's expensive and takes a lot of time. Just use the Yellow Pages."

So frustrating. But I was convinced that my idea would work.

A House Full of Women

In 1967, Little Odette turned ten, Dana turned five, and, in keeping with our every-five-years precedent, Zonia announced she was pregnant again. On September 2, she gave birth to Lisa Jacqueline, and we were thrilled to have her.

This same year, Big Odette married a man named Ruben from Chile, and they moved to Florida. That left me in the house with four females, and Zonia asked for a fifth. "I had a *Ninera* (nanny) named Paula when I was growing up in the White House in El Salvador," Zonia said. "Could we ask her to come and help take care of the girls and the house, now that Big Odette is gone?"

"Great idea," I said, and Paula was excited to come to America. We had only three bedrooms—one for Zonia and me, one for Little Odette, and one for Dana and Lisa, so we set up a bedroom for Paula in the basement.

Paula was wonderful with the children and looked so prim and proper with her gray hair combed back and the white jacket she always wore that made her look like a doctor. Zonia also liked to have someone in the house to go shopping with!

Before long, female number six surprised me. Tante Irma called. She told me that she had left Colorado after her son Gernot got married. For eighteen months she had lived in Los Angeles with Kotja, who taught at Cal State Northridge, and in Arizona, where she took various housekeeping jobs. At one point she worked for the Wrigley family, of chewing-gum fame.

Lisa, Dana, and Little Odette

"Why don't you come and live with us for a little while?" I asked. She came and stayed for four months and then returned to Gernot's in Colorado. While she lived with us she helped with the housekeeping and, of course, planted trees, bushes, and perennials around the yard. I had the best-looking gardens on the block!

FAMILY FUN

Our neighborhood overflowed with young children for Little Odette, Dana, and Lisa to play with. After school, they'd ride bikes, play hopscotch and play at the playground at Hampton Elementary. Dana was a tree climber—once I had to call the fire department because she wouldn't come down.

All three of the girls loved pets, so we always had a dog, rabbit, gerbil—you name it, we had one at some point.

Zonia made the kids' birthdays special. We invited their friends and our friends over for a party, and the birthday girl chose the dinner menu. Usually they asked for paella.

I played a lot of tennis at Clifton Park. Dana was only four when I started taking her with me and she liked to chase down the balls for me. As she got older I taught her to play.

Zonia and I were both used to traveling, and our family vacations reflected our love for taking trips. When the kids were very young we took them on day trips to Dutch Wonderland amusement park in Lancaster, Pennsylvania, and jaunts to the beach in Ocean City, Maryland. Zonia had friends in New York and would take the kids there for long weekends.

As the kids got older, our trips got longer. We drove several times to Florida to visit Zonia's relatives, and to Colorado Springs to visit Tante Irma. I had traded in my 1947 Chevy for a big red Oldsmobile Delta 88, and I'd load it up and hit the road. On our early trips, the interstate highway system wasn't completed so we'd drive ten hours through all the small towns, find a motel, and get up and do it again the next morning. It was slow going but a great way to see the country.

On the way to Colorado, the roads opened up when we hit Kansas and I'd barrel along at 80 miles an hour. We'd spend a couple of weeks visiting with Tante Irma, Gernot, and his wife, Ava. We hiked the Rockies and explored gold mines thousands of feet deep. Tante Irma always made her famous bean soup for me!

We were active as a family, and Zonia and I also found time to pursue our personal interests. Besides shopping, Zonia loved music and art—she was a talented painter. I chased action and adventure—like flying airplanes.

Chapter 16

COME FLY WITH ME

LUTHERVILLE, MARYLAND, USA
SAN JUAN, PUERTO RICO
1966-1974

AT A PARTY one weekend in the spring of 1966, my dentist friend Fabio got to talking about his fascination with airplanes. "I've always wanted to be a pilot," he said.

"Me too," I said, "ever since I flew to America."

"We should take lessons and get a pilot's license," Fabio suggested.

"Let's do it!" I said.

We checked around and called a small airport in Woodbine in Carroll County that offered flying lessons.

"Anytime you want to take a lesson, let us know and we'll set up a time," said the nice lady who owned the flight school. "We have six Piper two-seaters and two instructors."

Fabio and I picked a Saturday and reported to the office for our first lesson.

"Yes, Mr. Wurfl and Mr. Beltran. Welcome. Your instructors are flying with two other students right now but as soon as they come back, it'll be your turn. You can wait over in the hangar."

We waited and waited, then walked back to the office to check on the status.

"Where are the planes? We were supposed to start a half hour ago," we said.

"Sorry they're late," the lady said. "They should be in any minute."

Then the phone rang. It was the police. The two planes had collided in mid-air and crashed into the Liberty Reservoir. No one survived.

Fabio and I looked at each other. "Oh, my God. It could have been us," we said. "Let's go home and think about this a little more."

It took us a few months, but when Fabio and I got over the trauma, we talked again about taking flying lessons.

The school has been in business for years and that was the first accident.
It's a one-in-a-million thing.
You know what? We shouldn't let it stop us from flying. Let's go again!

After a couple of months, Fabio and I fulfilled our dreams and became licensed pilots.

Zonia was the first passenger I ever took for a ride. Once was enough for her. I took Dana, only four years old, for a flight and she loved it. She was too tiny to see anything out the windows so I'd prop her up with pillows and phone books. A lot of my friends also asked me to take them up for a ride, and sometimes I'd fly solo.

After flying for a while I took advanced lessons in navigating only by instruments so I'd be ready to fly in bad weather or any other situation where I couldn't see the ground. The instructor covered the windshield with a hood and taught me to take off, fly, and land the plane without relying on my eyes.

I rented planes out of Friendship Airport. They rented all kinds of planes and maintained them well so they were always flight-ready. Unlike the plane I once rented in Puerto Rico.

"I THINK I CAN MAKE IT!"

I had been flying for a few years, and one December, Zonia and I took a vacation with Fabio and his wife, Christine, to Puerto Rico between Christmas and New Year's. We stayed in San Juan at the El San Juan Hotel and made reservations for the New Year's Eve party at the Hunca Munca room there.

For lunch on New Year's Eve, we picked a place in Ponce, on the other side of the island. It would have been a long drive through mountains and rainforests, so I suggested we rent a plane and fly so we'd be sure to be back in time for the New Year's Eve party.

Halfway there, flying at 4,000 feet, beads of motor oil splash on the windshield. *Uh-oh.* Five minutes later, the engine—the one engine—sputters, and sputters some more, and conks out. Thank God these little planes don't nosedive, they glide. I glance at the map and we're only a few miles from a small airport near a town called Mayaguez.

"Are we going to make it?" everyone screams.

"Hold on! I see the runway! I think we can make it!" I said.

Almost. I land short of the runway in a sugarcane field. The sugar cane—eight feet tall and thick as baseball bats—slows down the plane and saves us from crashing. The razor-sharp sugarcane leaves slice the wheels off the plane and glass shatters everywhere.

The engine falls in my lap and I crawl out from under it, open the door, and help Zonia, Christine, and Fabio out of the cabin. They're bleeding a little from cuts on their arms and faces but otherwise don't seem to be hurt too badly. I don't have a scratch on me. An ambulance rushes to us, sirens blaring, and takes them to the hospital emergency room.

Our damaged plane after the emergency landing in Puerto Rico

For the next three hours, I'm grilled by the Federal Aviation Administration.

The ambulance returns with my passengers bandaged up here and there, but everyone is fine.

The four of us look around at one other. *What's the plan now?*

"We can still make it to the Hunca Munca party," I suggest.

"Okay, why not," everyone agrees.

"I'll ask if I can rent another plane," I say.

"*¡No más aviones alquilados! ¡Absolutamente no!*" ("No more rented planes! Absolutely not!") my passengers cry.

We took a commercial flight and partied in the new year.

"Dad, you've got nine lives," the girls said when I got home and told them the story.

Chapter 17

DIVERSIFIED

LUTHERVILLE, MARYLAND, USA, 1969-1985

IN 1969, I celebrated my 37th birthday and my 15th anniversary at Keiser & Keiser. I managed the entire agency but itched for something more. They paid me $20,000—a nice living but I believed I could fulfill my dream of owning my own business and make even more money along the way with my idea of selling through trade associations.

Neither would happen if I stayed at Keiser & Keiser. Klaus and Norman declined another request for an ownership stake in the company. I told them, "Okay, if that's the case, I'm going to have to think about what I'm going to do."

I talked to other agencies about acquiring stock in their companies; none were open to the idea. But in the course of my networking, I met a young independent insurance agent named Gary Hucek, who also happened to be Austrian, and we became friends.

Gary had a built-in pipeline of insurance business. His father-in-law was a wealthy real estate developer. Whenever he built a shopping center he would tell the construction companies bidding on the contract, "To win the job you have to give the insurance to my son-in-law."

Gary liked my idea of selling through trade associations, and we agreed that if we combined our diverse approaches, we could build a formidable agency together.

Starting a business with three children to feed was risky, but several factors propelled me forward. Mostly, I had confidence that I would succeed. I knew the industry from both sides—underwriting and sales—so I understood what insurance companies expected and how agencies acquired and retained customers.

I also had a financial head start with Gary's established pipeline, and my $600,000 book of annual premiums from Keiser & Keiser, which equates to nearly $3 million in 2023 dollars.

"Jack, it's not that easy," Norman warned me when I told him I was resigning to start my own agency. "When we started our business, we had roots in Baltimore that went way back. Over 50 contacts were ready to introduce us to leads. You weren't even born in this country. You have no family, and no network of college friends to help you get started.

"And there's fierce competition from big agencies who have been around a long time. Jack, you're not going to make it."

"You told me White Coffee Pot couldn't be done, and I did it. I'll start my agency in a different way, in my way," I said.

"Well, we hope you'll come back," Norman said. "That's your desk over there, and it will always be yours. You don't have to put your tail between your legs, just come back anytime you want and sit down."

The Coin-Op Laundry Association

Gary and I opened the office of the Diversified Insurance Industries at 10 East Fayette Street in downtown Baltimore on December 6, 1969. I thought long and hard about the name of the company. Most insurance agencies in those days were named after the owners, but no way I was going to be like everybody else and call it "Wurfl Insurance." I wanted to name it in a different way because I was going to sell insurance in a different way. I would sell to diverse groups of companies through trade associations in a diversity of industries. *That's it! Diversified Insurance Industries.*

Gary and I set up our desks, phones, paper, pencils, and typewriters (one was the new electric kind!), put our heads down, and started dialing. We printed business cards with the tagline, "Insurance for Associations."

In my travels around town, I noticed a flurry of innovative new retail establishments popping up all over. People who lived in apartments, which were also going up everywhere, would stuff bags full of their dirty laundry and drive to these "coin-op laundromats" in a nearby strip shopping center.

The laundromats were lined with rows of electric washing machines and dryers. Customers popped in a couple of quarters and sat down and read a magazine while they washed and dried their laundry.

Allright, a growth industry!

I scanned my list of trade associations and found one called the Maryland Coin-Op Laundry and Dry Cleaners Association. I called and asked them about insurance for their member companies. "It would really help us if you could endorse and write an insurance program for our members," the executive director said. "They have trouble finding affordable insurance. And if we offered insurance it would be another reason for a laundry to join the association."

The association gave me a list of its member companies, and each one told me a similar story. A doctor or lawyer would open a few laundromats as an investment but never set foot in the place to take care of it. Water would leak and a customer would fall and sue them. Or the circuits on the machines would overload, catch fire, and burn the place down. With such big losses, insurance companies either didn't want to go near them or would charge outrageous premiums.

Ah, the perfect prospects!

The first thing I did was advise the owners on how to reduce their losses: maintain and upgrade their machines, and hire an on-site attendant to fix equipment problems before they caused too much damage.

Next, I convinced a local insurance company, Harford Mutual in Bel Air, Maryland, to write coverage for a group of laundromats instead of individual laundromats, which spreads out the risk. "We'll give it a try for you, Jack," Harford Mutual said, "but only for operators in the state of Maryland."

That made my sales pitch easy. "Hello, I'm Jack Wurfl, Diversified Insurance. I'm the gentleman who now handles the insurance for the Maryland Coin-Op Laundry and Dry Cleaners Association. The executive director asked me to give you a call to show you how the association's program can increase your coverage and save you money." Almost everyone agreed to meet with me to hear more.

As I had predicted years before, the association members loved the idea.

The premium per location averaged only $600 or $700, but I sold dozens of policies at a time so the total premiums added up fast. I sold so many policies so quickly that I needed administrative help. I set up Zonia with a desk and a typewriter at home and she typed up policies in the evening.

Then I got a call from the Pennsylvania Coin-Op Laundry Association. "We hear you're writing insurance for laundries in Maryland. We'd like you to come to Pennsylvania and do the same thing here."

"Sure, I can do that."

And the Virginia association called and asked me to write coverage for laundry operators in their state.

Well, it looks like I need a national insurance company that can write in all 50 states.

I approached the Insurance Company of North America (INA), which is now called Cigna. I explained my strategy, showed them a list of my customers, and pitched the idea of writing policies for coin-op laundries throughout the country.

"You certainly know the industry," INA said. "We'll give it a try."

Growth Spurt

The pieces were now in place to sell across the country. We were poised to grow, and that's where my job satisfaction came from. Success was never a matter of money for me. I wanted to build something. That's my nature.

At the same time I was negotiating with INA, someone introduced me to Alfred Herwitz, a life insurance agent with Sun Life of Canada. "A lot of my clients are business owners," he told me. "They're always asking me about property and casualty insurance, and even their personal auto and homeowners insurance, but I can only sell life. How about we work out an agreement to refer leads to each other and go out together to sell bundles of policies?"

I thought teaming up with Al would be another good way to expand, and we worked out an agreement to exchange leads and split the commissions. With all the business owners I met through the Coin-Op Laundry Associations, our partnership was a win-win.

Backed by a national insurance underwriter, I hit the road to replicate my success with the Coin-Op Laundry Associations. In the next twelve months, I flew to 50 Insurance Company of North America offices around the country—about one per week. I explained my association sales strategy to the agents and paid Al to compile lists of coin-operated laundromats in their areas for me to give them.

Out of every 100 laundromats, the agents booked about 80 appointments and 40 sales. The closing rate blew my mind, especially since no one had ever tried this approach before. We barely kept our heads above water writing proposals for all the leads.

But why stop at Coin-Op Laundries?

We employed the same approach with the Electrical Association of America, the Plumbers Association, the Psychiatric Association, and all kinds of associations. INA formed a separate new company, MarketDyne International, with 200 agents focused on selling insurance to associations.

With agents in 50 offices to train, MarketDyne came up with a revolutionary idea to assure consistency to train the new agents they hired after I left. They called it a "video presentation."

They filmed the portion of my training session that covered the basics of how I started in association sales, how to find prospects, the most effective selling points to close a deal, and how much money they could make. They shipped televisions and video players to each office. After the video, I would answer questions.

I used a pile of laundry as a prop in my training video for agents selling to coin-operated laundry owners

Competitors noticed our success and copied our strategy, but that didn't bother us. We had more experience and knowledge, and we also majored in superior customer service. We were honest and fair and proposed insurance coverage that was best for the customer, not what generated the most profit for us. We checked in with customers several times a year—not once like most competitors—to make sure they were happy with their coverage and ask what else they needed from us.

Many of those customers are still with us today.

"We need more producers"

INA also came to Diversified to ask about additional insurance products we might need from them. Their marketing manager, Bill Tracy, called on me once or twice a year and we became friends as well as business colleagues.

On his visit in 1979, after we talked about how business was going at Diversified and INA, Bill lowered his voice and said, "You know, I think I might like to work on the agency side. I think I could make more money and have more flexibility and independence. Jack, do you think I would be successful in the agency business?"

"Yeah, I think so," I said, and asked him about his salary at INA. Diversified couldn't afford it unless he generated enough revenue to cover it, which was a risk because he had never sold anything before. But I liked his drive and customer-service mentality, and I could teach him to sell, so I told him I'd like to hire him and would discuss it with my partner.

I told Gary about Bill and asked him to cover a portion of Bill's salary out of his commissions. Gary said, "I like Bill, but no way I'm paying any of his salary. This is your idea. I don't need someone like him."

Gary had a different business philosophy than I did. He was satisfied with collecting the commissions that his father-in-law's referrals generated for him. I wanted to invest in the business and build something for the future.

One day we had a heart-to-heart talk about our differences. "Gary, your business will never grow the way you're doing things," I said. "We have to invest some of our commissions to hire more people to sell for us, like Bill Tracy."

Gary just didn't want to do that, and after ten years together, we worked out an amicable agreement to end our business partnership.

When I told Al about Bill, he said, "I'd be happy to pay part of his salary if that's what it takes to hire him."

"We would like to become part of Diversified"

Later in 1979, a growth opportunity came from a most unlikely source. I had kept in touch with my colleagues at Keiser & Keiser since I left ten years before, but I never dreamed Norman Keiser would ever call and say, "Keiser & Keiser isn't doing well at all, and you are doing so great. We're not going to make it without you. So we want to ask if you would either come back here and take over, or buy us and we'll become part of Diversified."

I bought their family agency and folded their dozen employees and their entire book of business into Diversified. By 1983 we needed more office space and moved to the Village of Cross Keys, a cozy mix of offices, boutique shops, and eateries on Falls Road in Baltimore near East Northern Parkway.

All of my new staff embraced the association sales strategy, and by the mid-1980s Diversified wrote insurance for 160 different associations and our annual premiums reached $100 million.

Chapter 18

PIED PIPER

LUTHERVILLE, MARYLAND, USA, 1969-1985

As THE GIRLS and Diversified grew, our family took longer and farther vacations. I've lost count of how many times we've been to Disney World. Little Odette, Dana, and Lisa carried around their autograph books for Mickey and Minnie and all the other characters to sign. We ate breakfast with Donald and Daisy, rode through "It's a Small World," where we especially enjoyed the Spanish and German versions, and beamed at the shows and parades.

Summers in El Salvador became a tradition. Zonia and the girls stayed from June until August. I joined them a couple of times and stayed for two or three weeks. The girls loved seeing their grandparents and playing with their pet chickens. They also spent a week with their *Tia Concha Bella* (Aunt Concha Bella) and laughed at her parrot, who spoke Spanish and expanded their vocabularies with a few choice curse words!

The houses in El Salvador are built for the hot weather. All the floors are tiled to keep the house cool. My favorite feature was the open courtyard with no roof smack in the middle of the house.

The beaches were beautiful. One was unlike anything I had ever seen. The whole beach was black from the volcanic ash mixed in the sand. But it was delightful! So soft, like walking in flour. We took walks and passed what looked like palm trees growing on the beach but they were banana plants. We never saw any beaches like that in Ocean City!

The black sand felt like flour under our feet
Photo credit: Wikimedia Commons, David Oviera

    I spent a lot of my time with Zonia's friends Alfredo and Martita Batlle, who were one of the largest coffee growers in the country. They owned a house near Lake Coatepeque, and Alfredo took their daughter Cecilia, and my girls out in his boat. Alfredo, a Johns Hopkins graduate, owned motorcycles, and one year he and I rode up the Pan American Highway for two days through El Salvador and Guatemala. I fell over only a few times; never anything serious, just a few scrapes.

    Zonia's relatives and friends were well-to-do—no surprise when you're related to the former president—but our travels sometimes took us through poor areas of San Salvador, the capital city. I thought seeing the poverty and homelessness helped Little Odette, Dana, and Lisa realize that there are people less fortunate who need a helping hand.

"Would you help me move to America?"

When Zonia's oldest brother, Edmundo, saw how happy and successful his big sisters Zonia and Big Odette were in the United States, he wanted to follow in their footsteps. He realized that his opportunities in El Salvador were limited since his uncle had been out of office for so long. "Would you help me move to America?" he asked me

"Of course," I said.

I filled out all the immigration paperwork and pledged my personal assets as a guarantee that he would never become a financial burden to the U.S. government. I paid for his flight to Baltimore and he lived with us when he first arrived. We had space for him because Paula, our housekeeper from El Salvador, had moved back home around 1974 when both she and the kids were older.

Edmundo spoke no English, but one of my customers, Comfy Manufacturing, was hiring production workers and didn't require them to speak English so he could start work right away. Except he needed transportation. The timing worked out perfectly because my partner, Gary, was ready to trade in his old car. I bought it from him and gave it to Edmundo.

It didn't take long for Edmundo to feel financially stable enough to move into an apartment, especially since living with his older sister and her husband and kids cramped his social life. So did school. I signed him up for the same English classes for adults that I had taken at night at Baltimore City College High School but he quit after three weeks. He preferred to go to parties at night and meet girls.

About a year later, Zonia's next brother, Roberto, saw how well Edmundo was doing and called me. "Could you help me come to America too?"

"Of course," I said, and I repeated the process: the immigration paperwork and financial guarantee, a flight to Baltimore, a place to sleep in our house, a job at Comfy Manufacturing, and a car. And, just like his brother, Roberto quit English classes at City after a few weeks and moved into an apartment as soon as he could.

Another year or two passed and, right on cue, Zonia's third brother, Rene, called me. A few weeks later he was sleeping at our house, working at Comfy Manufacturing, and driving a used car. After a few more weeks he dropped out of night school and moved into an apartment.

I was three for three! And proud that they all became U.S. citizens.

But now, Zonia's parents were alone in El Salvador. That didn't last long.

"We'd like to come to America to be with our children and grandchildren," they said.

"Of course," I said.

We set them up in an apartment on Argonne Drive, and I enjoyed having Zonia's whole family close to us.

There was only one family member I ever turned down.

"Don't even think about coming to Baltimore"

My brother Peter had been living in South Africa for over twenty years with his wife Anita and their two daughters, Astrid and Karen. Neither Astrid nor Karen wanted to live anymore in a country with an official policy of racial separation. "Maybe you're used to it," they told Peter, "but we have to leave."

Peter and Anita thought they should all move as a family, and Peter called to tell me that he was leaving South Africa.

"Well, where are you going?" I asked.

He said, "I think I'm coming back to the United States."

"Really? Going back to New York?"

"No, I want to come to Baltimore."

"Why Baltimore?" I asked. "You said it's a hick town."

"Because I'm going to work at Diversified," he said.

I laughed. "Peter, it's a lovely thought, but I don't think it would be a good idea for us to work together."

"Why not?"

"We would never get along."

I hurt my brother's feelings yet again, but it turned out to be the best decision for him. He and his family moved to Australia and established a nice life for themselves.

Chapter 19

PLAY HARD

LUTHERVILLE, MARYLAND, USA
THE COAST OF SOUTH AMERICA
1972-PRESENT

I'VE ALWAYS BELIEVED that you work hard, but you play hard too. Playing hard is the pleasure payoff from working hard, and makes the work worthwhile.

When you're playing hard you're also learning something new, and I love learning. After I learned to fly an airplane, I took advanced instruction and learned how to fly blind—by instruments only—so that I'd be ready to fly in unexpected bad weather or any other emergencies where I couldn't see the ground. The instructor covered the windshield with a hood and taught me how to take off, cruise, and land the plane without seeing anything out the windshield.

In 1972, after flying for six years, I had learned all I could and itched for a new hobby to try. I scratched that itch at a dinner party when an attorney friend of mine introduced me to Bill Donovan, who trained thoroughbred racehorses. I've loved horses ever since I plowed the fields behind them in Dangast, so I enjoyed talking horses with Bill.

He told me all about the horse-racing world and I said, "That sounds like fun. Can you recommend a horse for me to buy?" A few weeks later Bill took me to a stable to look at one named The Preacher. Bill told me why he liked him, and that was good enough for me.

*The Preacher won at Laurel in 1972. I'm standing,
third from the left. Bill, my trainer, is fifth from the left.*

"How much?" I asked.

"Two thousand dollars," Bill said.

"I'll take him."

Bill liked to train The Preacher early in the morning before the other trainers arrived so nobody else could clock his speed. I'd have to be in the stands at 7 am if I wanted to observe.

My family, friends, and customers got the biggest kick out of coming to the track at Pimlico or Laurel or Bowie or Timonium to see The Preacher race and betting $2 on him. At Laurel on October 16, 1972, we all won! The bad news is, The Preacher never won another race.

Fast Hero was my second horse, and he won a race at Bowie in February 1973. In May, Secretariat, who had won the Kentucky Derby, moved into the barn next to us during Preakness week. Secretariat trained at 7 am, the same time we trained Fast Hero, so I met his owner, Penny Chenery. What a wonderful lady. We sat together and watched our horses. Fast Hero never came close to "Big Red's" times, so Penny was willing to chat about horses with me. Some days we'd eat lunch together in the dining room, and she was generous with her advice about horse training.

Secretariat won the Preakness in record time and won horse racing's Triple Crown that year. Penny Chenery syndicated him for $6 million. Fast Hero turned out to be another one-hit wonder, but that's more than I can say about my third horse, Capsiculia, who never found the winner's circle.

For me and my wagering friends, racing horses was a fun but expensive hobby.

BACK TO THE SEA

My hobbies had taken me to the air and the land. One more domain to go—my first love, the sea.

From the time they were four or five years old, Little Odette, Dana, and Lisa all loved the water, whether swimming in the Atlantic Ocean at Ocean City or in the Pacific off of El Salvador, or fishing in the Chesapeake Bay. We enjoyed it so much—so did Zonia every once in a while—that in 1972 I bought a 27-foot, single-engine Silverton that I christened *Gretel*, after my mother.

By the time she became a teenager, Dana was an expert pilot and my first mate. She'd steer most of the time while the rest of us fished with our rods and reels.

After a few years, I upgraded to a 40-foot Post, a twin-engine sport fisherman boat with a tuna bridge on top, a full kitchen, a full bathroom,

Play Toy

and two staterooms with three beds. I named her *Play Toy*. The kids loved it.

So did my seafaring customers, which helped my business. The insurance industry is all about building relationships. Customers called me and asked, "Jack, when are you going to take me fishing?" I took them as soon as possible because once they climbed aboard they wanted to be my crew members for life.

The manager at the Insurance Company of North America was one of my biggest fishing fans. He held our monthly agency meetings on my boat, and who can blame him? None of his other agencies sailed him to St. Michaels and discussed business over steamed crabs and beer.

Lisa and Camelot Farms

My investment in horses took a different turn in 1974 on a visit to Tante Irma in Colorado. On the final leg of the drive there, Lisa's face lit up when she saw a group of kids riding horses at the Garden of the Gods nature center in Colorado Springs.

"Dad, can we do that?" she asked.

"Yeah, we'll be here for a couple of weeks, so we'll do it."

Ever since the day she got on a horse—at seven years old—riding was all she wanted to do. As soon as we got home from Colorado she asked me, "Dad, where can I ride around here?"

Zonia took Lisa for riding lessons at the Dayspring farm in Jacksonville almost every day after school, until Dana got her driver's license and took over transportation duty. When I was convinced she was going to stick with it, I bought her a horse, named Razmataz. I stabled Razmataz at my good friend and client Phil Spector's barns at nearby Camelot Farms.

Phil had asked me to buy into Camelot Farms as a partner but I didn't have time for cleaning stalls, painting fences, and cutting

Lisa won a box full of ribbons!

grass. But I helped Phil with the chores when I could, boarded my horse there, and hired his instructor for Lisa's riding lessons.

Lisa advanced from riding around the ring at Dayspring to competing in horse shows. As her riding skills improved I sold Razmataz and bought a stronger, more spirited horse named Jumping Juniper. Almost every weekend for the next decade we woke up at 5 am, loaded our horse on the trailer, and drove off to shows up and down the East Coast. Dana came with us a few times, and Lisa won a box full of ribbons.

Saddle Up

Around 1984, shortly after Dana graduated from college, the two of us were watching Lisa ride at a show and Dana said, "You know what, Dad? We should take riding lessons."

"You're right, let's do it," I said. The timing was perfect because Lisa would soon be away at college and no longer riding.

On the hunt with Phil Spector

I called Phil and signed up for lessons at Camelot. At age 52 I grabbed the reins and put my safety in the hands of an eighteen-year-old instructor named Renee. Phil had never ridden either and he took lessons with Dana and me. Dana rode Jumping Juniper, and I bought a horse for myself, Toby. Renee didn't waste any time getting the three of us trotting, cantering, and jumping—my sweet spot was a three-foot oxer.

I loved the challenge! The exhilaration! And the cool down. After our lessons, we'd hike one of the trails on the farm and end the day relaxing with wine and cheese while the moon rose.

After a few months, I could gallop and let go of the reins, and raise my arms in the air. Renee then taught us the highest form of flat riding, called dressage. Dressage is like ballet on horseback, with complicated lateral moves like shoulder-in and half-pass. But for all of dressage's elegance, Phil and I got bored with riding in a confined area. "Let's go for a trail ride," I said. Dana hesitated, but she followed us on a gallop through the woods.

"Well, I survived," Dana said with a sigh of relief when we returned to the barn. "Dodging all those branches was *loaaads* of fun."

But Phil wanted more challenges. He joined the Pretty Boy Hunt Club in Hampstead and persuaded me to hunt with him. "I'm not shooting any foxes," Dana said. She came with us once and followed behind our horses hostessing the stirrup cups and serving drinks.

Linked

Around 1985, after more than a decade as a boat owner, I had so many customers who wanted me to take them fishing that I was on my boat every Saturday at 6 am. That meant I left my house at 5 am to drive an hour to the Piney Narrows marina, just over the Chesapeake Bay Bridge on Kent Island. I'd gas up the boat—$200 worth—load the food, drinks, and ice, and set out fishing rods and bait for ten or fifteen people.

Yes, the outings were good for business, but I grew tired of all the work. One of my fellow boat-owner friends, the claims manager at the Insurance Company of North America, felt the same pain. One day while we were out fishing we talked about selling our boats. "I'd love to sell it," I said, "but what would I do instead for fun?"

He said, "Jack, if you're looking for a new hobby, I have two sets of golf clubs in my car. Let's go to the golf course right now and you can try it."

I played my first round at Pine Ridge near my house, and I was surprised by how much I enjoyed chasing a little white ball around. I practiced just about every night at Pine Ridge and became friendly with the Towson University student who worked in the pro shop, named Tom Carroll.

One evening I said to Tom, "You work here in the pro shop, so why don't you play once in a while?"

"I've taken some lessons on the driving range," he said, "but I lose all the balls in the trees."

I finally got him to go with me one night, and from the first tee, he drove the ball twice as far as I ever hit it.

I couldn't wait to get Dana onto the course. We enjoyed horseback riding together, so why not golf?

"Let me take you out on the driving range at Pine Ridge," I suggested.

She was game, and after a few times on the range, I told her, "I think you're ready to play a round."

"Okay!" she said.

"But you can't go out without a golf glove," I said. "Let's get one from the pro shop and then we'll play."

Dana picked out a glove and walked up to the counter. Tom and another guy who worked in the pro shop flipped a coin to decide who would be the lucky one to wait on her. Tom won the toss. Dana paid Tom for the glove and, while she headed out to the first tee, I hung back and chatted for a minute with Tom.

As we took our practice swings on the first tee, I told Dana. "That guy who sold you the glove, he's a friend of mine. We've played together in the evening after he gets off work. He's going to play with us if he can. His name is Tom Carroll."

Dana was never madder at me than at that moment. On the third hole, she was lining up a putt when Tom rode up in a golf cart. He was all smiles and cordial; Dana was fuming. But Tom was so nice that by the end of the round, Dana asked Tom if he could play with us again the next evening. And the next evening. The three of us played almost every day after work.

"AWESTRUCK"

Other than Jack's immediate family, I don't know if he has impacted anyone else's life trajectory more profoundly than mine.

I was approaching my senior year at Towson University, a kid just trying to find his way in the world. I wanted to escape the financial uncertainty that I grew up under, and I felt that if I ever got a break, I would throw myself into the opportunity and give the best version of myself to it.

I was looking for advice and struck up a relationship with a wise and friendly gentleman who came into the Pine Ride pro shop quite often to rent a pull cart. I saw that he drove a Mercedes so I knew he was successful. What Jack liked to do was play a few holes with me until dark, and occasionally we'd go Ocean Pride on York Road and eat a crab or two. I had no money, so getting dinner out of the deal appealed to me.

Jack loved to talk about his hobbies. I learned all about his fishing and flying, his racehorses, and when he took up golf. *Could I ever have a life like that?* As our friendship grew closer, he started to share some of his childhood history, and became larger than life to me. I was starry-eyed; mesmerized.

Jack also shared stories about his business and asked me what I had planned after graduation. I was an accounting and finance major, thinking about accounting or banking. I laid out my thoughts to Jack one evening, and he said, "You know, Tom, I've done very well in insurance. You seem like a nice, personable young man. Smart enough. I think you could do well in insurance also." So now I had another career track to consider.

Then one day, Jack walks into the pro shop with Dana, and I'm awestruck by how beautiful she is. I sell her a golf glove, and she pays no attention to me. But when Jack asks me to play with them, inside I'm jumping up and down and thinking, *Holy cow, this is great!* It could have started thundering and lightning, or a hurricane or tornado could have blown through, but I was going out to play with them!

I didn't have much of a golf game at the time, and I didn't

> know what to talk to Dana about, but my love language is "acts of service," so I became a world-class young gentleman. I encouraged Dana on every shot, picked up her extra clubs from around the green, and fetched her ball out of the cup.
>
> The three of us played almost every night over the next few weeks. Sometimes Dana's boyfriend joined us—a good-looking guy who I liked a lot, though I secretly hoped he would go away.
>
> I kept up my gentlemanly demeanor, and Dana noticed. One evening, I handed her a club and she said, "Are you for real?" That was the first glimmer of hope that I had a chance with Dana. It happened on the third fairway at Pine Ridge. I'll never forget it as long as I live.
>
> —Tom Carroll

On the links in Hawaii with moon golfer Alan Shepard

Over the months and years, Dana got hooked on golf and hooked on Tom. He was so intelligent, and I liked him so much that I offered him a job at Diversified. Dana liked him so much they got married in 1990.

I joined the Caves Valley Golf Club in Owings Mills, and over the next 40 years, I played golf all over the U.S., at the St. Andrews Old Course in Scotland, in Ireland, and too many other places to name. I shoot mostly in the low 90s, which is why I recommend taking up golf when you're five, not fifty. But better late than never.

The Hartford insurance company

invited me to play in a tournament in Hawaii where the guest of honor was the astronaut Alan Shepard, the only man ever to hit a golf ball on the moon. I had the privilege of playing a round and riding in a golf cart with him.

Never in my wildest dreams did I think playing golf would land me at the Supreme Court. In 1976, I went by myself to play one evening and was put in a group with law students. I was much older but we enjoyed playing together and met up several times over the summer.

One of the students, Linda Cawley, aspired to offer legal services at below-standard rates for people who couldn't afford typical legal fees. Instead of charging $350 for a simple will she wanted to charge $35. That meant she needed a high volume of work to sustain a practice. Her strategy for generating the volume was to advertise her services. There was just one problem: the state Bar Association banned advertising by lawyers.

When Linda graduated, I lent her $2,000 to open her first clinic on Eastern Avenue in Baltimore, and she sued the Bar Association to strike down the advertising ban. In 1977, her case escalated all the way to the Supreme Court, and she invited me to attend the hearing.

When I stepped into the United States Supreme Court Building in Washington, D.C., it was my first time ever in any courtroom. I sat on the edge of my seat as Linda and her opponent presented their arguments and the justices grilled them with questions. Fabulous!

Linda won the case, pioneered legal-services advertising, and opened over a dozen affordable legal clinics in Maryland. I came away with greater respect and confidence in our judicial system.

Cap'n Jack

I loved golf, and I didn't miss the hassles of owning a boat, but I missed fishing. My good fishing buddy and customer Larry Cohen suggested a solution: The two of us could hire a private charter and crew for a deep-sea-fishing trip every year.

That sounded great to me, but where? Ocean City was a convenient location, but did we want to waste time sailing out 60 miles or more to reach the deeper, warmer waters where the big fish are?

"Costa Rica is the place to go," Larry said. And he was right. Ten or twenty miles out and we were in deep, deep water, and the big fish were right there. Over the next few years, we fished out of different ports up and down Costa Rica.

> ### A Hike in the Jungle
>
> Jack got his sea legs early, as a boy in Germany. The North Sea gets pretty rough, so he knew what he was doing on our bill fishing trips to the Pacific off of South America. The 50-pound roosterfish he caught in the Bat Islands off Costa Rica was one of the most gorgeous fish I've seen.
>
> On our trips we normally fished every other day, so we enjoyed some unique experiences off the boat on the in-between days. In Panama, we signed up for a hike with a local outfitter. We boarded a twin-engine plane and landed on a narrow strip on the edge of the Darién Gap jungle.
>
> From there we rode in a cart hooked up to a tractor that jostled us to the edge of a river. We climbed in a rowboat that ran us down to a Panamanian Indian village. The locals tried to sell us their wares but we just watched the dancing.
>
> We trekked two and a half hours deep into the jungle and stopped at a waterfall. The blue butterflies that fluttered up and down the falls mesmerized us. We took a swim under the falls, ate lunch, and hiked another two and a half hours back to the rowboat. We made a voyage that, according to our guide, only two or three other tourists have ever taken.
>
> —Larry Cohen

Our group of fishermen, the frequency of our trips, and our destinations all expanded over the next 30 years.

A friend of Larry's, Mark Levy, who owned several pharmacies around Baltimore, started fishing with us in the late 1990s. In 2007, as Larry stood in line to make dinner reservations on his Caribbean vacation cruise, he got to talking about our fishing trips with the man in front of him, a retired three-star general from Monterey, California, named Robert Ord.

"I would love to do something like that," General Ord told Larry. "Could I go with you guys sometime?" Bob has fished with us ever since and has become one of my dearest friends.

Soon, one trip a year wasn't enough. We upped it to twice a year, and sometimes three. We fished together so often we called ourselves "The Four Amigos" and made up nicknames for everybody.

General Ord's nickname was obvious—we called him "The General." Mark, who owned the pharmacies, was "The Doctor." The General dubbed Larry "The Gunner," because he always bragged about the time he fired a 50-caliber machine gun at a military exhibition. And they called me "The Captain" because they said I helped them a lot with their fishing. But I don't know about that; I think we all helped one another.

The Four Amigos return to Cabo San Lucas harbor in 2013.
Left to Right: The Captain, The Doctor, The Gunner, and The General

As we increased our number of expeditions we looked for new waters. We fished off various ports in Panama and Mexico and fell in love with Cabo San Lucas off the southern tip of Mexico's Baja California Sur.

Bob kept a log of all the trips he took with us. By his count, over those dozen years we caught a total of 59 marlin. My biggest weighed 410 pounds. But for us, fishing was about getting away from it all and the thrill of the hunt, not a seafood dinner. We released every fish we caught.

Life was totally different on the water, and I loved it. I didn't even think about my business the whole week. We averaged about seven catches per trip, but whether we caught anything or not, every day was carefree and relaxing. "Not seeing land is a hoot," Bob Ord always said. We did whatever we wanted and went wherever we wanted. Freedom! The way I felt as a kid on the North Sea, away from the Gestapo and the SS.

"I'D WANT JACK IN MY FOXHOLE"

I met Jack for the first time on March 15, 2007, at the airport in Cabo San Lucas, where we gathered for our fishing trip. When Jack, Mark, Larry, and I got to our villa, it was locked and the real estate agent was nowhere in sight. Somehow he forgot about us.

We walked around the back and spotted an open window on the second floor. The three of them looked at me and their faces all said, *You might be a retired Lieutenant General, but now you're just another one of the guys and have to earn your stripes as the newbie. Climb your ass up there, General!* I climbed through the window and let them in the front door.

Every time we got together we told stories from the time we hopped in the rental car at the airport until we returned it at the end of the week. We told the same stories over and over but that didn't stop us from laughing out loud all week.

Jack was the consummate team player. Pulling in a 200-pound marlin on a boat that's rocking and rolling is a challenge. But

> Jack has that tough German-Austrian blood in him, and he was never the guy who needed help. He was the one who always helped the rest of us.
>
> Whenever the boat got wobbly as I moved from the cabin to the fighting chair, Jack would hustle over and walk behind me to steady me. Then as the fish thrashed back and forth in the water he'd turn the chair to keep me lined up with it. His physical strength and inner strength amazed me.
>
> Jack was damn good in the fighting chair himself. It's not easy to wrestle a fish for 20 or 30 minutes, but he never backed down and almost always reeled them in. It's a glorious experience and he reveled in it.
>
> Jack is tough as nails, but he's also compassionate, caring, and loving. He puts other people ahead of himself. After I had my quadruple open-heart bypass surgery he was one of the first friends to call me.
>
> Jack and I will always be fellow soldiers. If our country had to go to war again, I'd want Jack in my foxhole.
>
> —Lieutenant General Robert Ord
> U.S. Army (Retired)

LIFETIME SPORTS

Hobbies came and went, but I played two sports for most of my lifetime.

I've skied since I was a boy on wooden skis in Austria, and didn't stop until I reached my eighties. I taught Dana and Lisa to ski and they couldn't wait for our winter trips to Colorado. There's no rush like the rush you get looking out from the top of a mountain, and then *whoosh*, down you go.

I started playing tennis in the army and continued on the clay courts at Clifton Park in Baltimore. My game reached a new level in 2003 when I played mixed doubles with pros Maria Sharapova, Andy Roddick, and Ashley Harkleroad.

The Rouse Company, which owned our office building, sponsored Pam Shriver's annual fundraising tennis exhibition. Pam, aka "The Legend of Lutherville," is a tennis Hall of Famer who is Dana's age and grew up in our neighborhood.

With Ashley Harkleroad, Andy Roddick, and Maria Sharapova

Diversified was the largest tenant in the building, which earned me VIP access to the professional players at the tournament, including Pam and Andy Roddick. I teamed up for doubles with Harkleroad against Sharapova, then only sixteen years old, and James Blake.

I couldn't return a single ball that Sharapova hit to me unless she eased up on it, and she kindly let me hit a few winners past her. But I've always taken credit for being a valuable practice partner for her—she beat Serena Williams to win Wimbledon the following summer.

LIFE BALANCE

Playing hard is equally as important as working hard. You push your limits and prove to yourself that you can do almost anything. You mature in your relationships with other people when you play fair and by the rules. Life balance and physical activity make you a happier person and a more productive worker.

I couldn't have found the balance without Zonia's dedication to raising our children and the many times she played hard and took them to El Salvador and on other trips while I stayed home.

Nor could I have struck a balance without three daughters who balanced playing with me on the slopes, tennis courts, airplanes, boats, and horses, all the while working so hard in school. Little Odette graduated from Towson High

School as a special-needs student. The state of Maryland appointed someone to help her find a job, but after they searched for almost a year with no results, I decided to look myself.

I asked around among my friends and customers and one said, "I think I have a connection for you. My wife is the secretary to the head of the Social Security Administration. She can ask if anything is available." Social Security hired her and she worked there for ten years.

Lisa graduated from Towson High and majored in Communications and Branding at the University of Maryland. After college, she began her career in advertising, branding, graphic design, and web design. She has worked for advertising agencies and as an independent consultant.

Dana played *and* worked with me. From the time she was ten years old, she loved to go into the office with me on Saturday mornings—when we weren't fishing or at a horse show—and help me open the boxes of mail that had piled up during the week. Dana called it "fun, fun, fun" and I enjoyed having her with me.

The summer after ninth grade at Towson High, Dana asked, "Dad, can I come to the office and work with you?" I said, "Sure!" She worked with me every summer throughout high school and her college years at the University of Maryland, which makes her the first in a steady stream of loyal, long-term employees at Diversified.

Chapter 20

OFF-BALANCE

LUTHERVILLE, MARYLAND, USA, 1987-2003

WE CAN TRY to maintain a balance in life, but there are always disruptions beyond our control.

In the late 1980s, when Zonia and I were both in our late fifties, I noticed how often she forgot things. She also seemed anxious much of the time and had trouble sleeping.

What can I do for her? How can I show her how much I love her?

On the spur of the moment one day, I drove over to a new development on Seminary Farm Road, only ten minutes away. I looked at one of the houses for sale, number 73. *This is it! What a great surprise for Zonia!* I made a deal with the builder on the spot.

One day when we were running errands together, I told Zonia I had to drop off an insurance policy to a customer. I pulled up to 73 Seminary Farm Road. "What do you think of this house?" I asked her.

"It's beautiful!" she said.

"Well, it's yours!"

AWFUL DISEASES

Zonia loved the new house, but her forgetfulness, anxiety, and sleep disorder worsened. We told her doctor, and he was quick to prescribe sleeping pills and anxiety medication. In retrospect, maybe too quick.

Zonia became dependent on the medications. Worse, she secretly asked a friend of hers from El Salvador, who owned a pharmacy in Florida, to send her more pills. By the time I discovered that she was overmedicating herself and warned her of the danger, it was too late for her to wean herself off of what she was taking.

She struggled for a few years and a psychiatrist finally found the root of the problem. She was diagnosed with dementia, which progressed to Alzheimer's disease. Dana, Lisa, and I did the best we could to take care of her, but dementia and Alzheimer's are awful, and even worse when they attack someone in their fifties who has been misdiagnosed for years. There was nothing anyone could do to reverse her decline.

Then, in 1992, I was diagnosed with colon cancer.

After my surgery, I faced months of radiation and chemotherapy. After struggling at home for two years to take care of myself and Zonia, Dana insisted that I move in with her and Tom. "You can't take care of Mom, and Mom can't take care of you," she said. She and Lisa would help Zonia.

That arrangement worked so well that I lived with Dana and Tom for nine years, until they moved to a new home in February 2003. We all pitched in to take care of Zonia, but Alzheimer's had slowly disabled her, both mentally and physically.

Later in 2003, Zonia called me in a panic. "Jack, I fell in the kitchen and my arm is bleeding. I can't get up." I raced home. Zonia had managed to get off the floor and into bed. I cringed when I saw the bone sticking out of her arm.

I realized that we could no longer leave Zonia alone. I called a home care agency, and they sent a steady flow of caregivers to work various shifts so that Zonia received around-the-clock care. Some of the caregivers were terrific, others not so much. And I didn't like the parade of people coming and going in and out of the house.

I happened to mention the situation to Sal DiPietro at lunch one day. "What I really need," I said, "is someone to live with us and take care of Zonia."

"You know what?" Sal said. "We have a babysitter, and she has a friend who's also a babysitter. Sometimes the friend brings her kids over to play with my kids. But now she's looking for another job because the family she worked for moved away."

Nohemy (standing) fixes a salad for Zonia

"Tell me about her," I said. "Do you like her? What's her name?"

"She's terrific," Sal said. "Our kids loved playing with her kids, and we were always glad when she came over."

"She sounds good," I said.

"Her name is Nohemy. It's a Latin name. She's from El Salvador."

"Oh, my God. El Salvador! This is a perfect match!"

Dana, Lisa, and I loved Nohemy from the moment we met her. She had other job offers but came to live with us and she took care of Zonia like she was her own mother.

Chapter 21

THE LOYALTY EFFECT

LUTHERVILLE, MARYLAND, USA
ALASKA, ITALY, FRANCE, AUSTRIA, CZECH REPUBLIC
1969-PRESENT

I LOVED PLAYING hard, and I loved working hard. My biggest worry in life was whether there would be enough work for me in this world. I was so eager to sink my teeth into my own company and accomplish and build something, not only for myself, but for my family, my employees, and my customers.

My worry quickly disappeared. I found enough work to do when I opened Diversified. I enjoyed every minute, and Diversified grew into one of the 200 largest insurance agencies in the country.

Some of our growth came through additional mergers. I was so busy I didn't have time to seek mergers, but like Keiser & Keiser, the J. Ramsey Barry agency, one of the largest in Baltimore at the time, called and said, "You're doing so well and we're struggling. Would you take us over?" The Jerry Cohen agency called and asked, "Can we come in and work through Diversified?" I agreed to both, and over the years acquired additional smaller agencies in the same way.

Agents (aka "producers") from other agencies also called and said, "I'm not happy where I am now. Could I come to Diversified and bring all my business?" I'd evaluate them and, if I thought they were a good fit, bring them on board.

We grew organically also. Not as many people went to college in the early years of the business, so I have people working here who I hired 40 years ago out of high school. We're committed to offering extensive training to our employees so they have opportunities to advance in the company.

Happy and engaged employees attract other happy and engaged employees. In 1981 I hired a high school graduate, Phyllis Jeddry, as an assistant bookkeeper. A couple of years later I hired her sister, Karen Wladkowski, as a receptionist. They've both stayed with us for over 40 years and worked their way up to become vice presidents.

Karen keeps me organized nowadays and I always joke with her, "I hired you decades ago and now I work for you!" Since their father died, Phyllis and Karen tell me that they think of me as their second father now.

Years ago, one of my salesmen, Henry, asked me if I would meet with his friend Aaron Margolies, who sold life insurance but was interested in moving into property and casualty. "I'll train him," Henry said.

"I'd be happy to talk to him," I said.

I hired Aaron, and Henry began training him but took half of his commissions. "I'll go out on your sales calls with you," I told Aaron, "and you can keep the entire commission." After a year or so he didn't need me to go with him anymore. Aaron has been selling for us for over 30 years and has landed some of our largest accounts.

We started selling through trade associations, but each producer has total freedom to build their portfolio with whatever type of business they like, so our customer base expanded and evolved. Many of our salesmen are industry experts and can talk to those prospects and customers about the best practices for their company, which gives them a leg up on competitors.

I feel a lot of satisfaction when people like Phyllis, Karen, and Aaron learn new skills, take on more responsibilities, and advance rapidly within the company. "Rocketeers," they're known as around the office. Growth opportunity is why we have so many people who have stayed with us for such a long time—about 40 percent of our employees have between ten and 40-plus years of tenure.

We celebrate employee loyalty and longevity. We print everyone's start date on their nameplate and recognize members of the Decade Club, which employees join on their tenth anniversary. Every year we treat Decade Club members to a special luncheon at a nice restaurant or a crab feast on a charter boat in Annapolis, and they receive a Christmas bonus of a week's pay.

A Family Business

I'm proud to say that I've worked with all three of my daughters at Diversified.

After working at the Social Security Administration, Little Odette joined us in 1983 and worked for ten years as a mail clerk. She left after she married David James in 1993 and moved to Gettysburg, Pennsylvania.

Dana worked weekends and summers at the office with me starting when she was ten, and has never worked anywhere except at Diversified. When she was in high school, I started taking her everywhere with me and introduced her to my customers. She entered the University of Maryland with the idea of pursuing a medical career but came home during her sophomore year with an announcement.

"Dad, I want to tell you something. I changed my major."

"To what?"

"Business."

"Why did you do that?"

"Because I'd like to go into business with you!"

That was Mozart music to my ears! Dana has been working full-time at Diversified since she graduated in 1984.

Lisa has worked with us on a consulting basis since she opened her own graphic design firm in 2001. She handles our website, promotion, and social media.

Loyal Employees = Loyal Customers

Our loyal employees have brought in loyal customers. Our biggest challenge is intense competition, as Norman Keiser warned me in 1969. Diversified has always stood apart from the competition through strong relationships.

We start with honesty, fairness, and putting customers' insurance interests ahead of our commissions. Then we check in with each customer multiple times a year—the practice I started when I founded the company—to find out if they have any problems and if they need any additional insurance. This way we can design solutions for them that a competitor who calls them once a year might miss.

As a result, we've kept many of our customers since my video presentation days in the 1970s. They're friends, not just customers. I have two very large customers who have grandsons working for Diversified.

> ### COMFORTABLE WITH JACK
>
> I don't remember how I got Jack's name, but I needed insurance for my clothing manufacturing business and I called him. We met in my office on May 9, 1977, at 4 pm. Jack and his assistant, Karen, laugh that I remember the precise date and time, but Jack has verified it from his appointment book.
>
> I was impressed with Jack's calm demeanor and felt comfortable with him. He never pushed me to buy. I can read people and could tell that Jack was honest and that he knew what he was talking about. I didn't need to shop for any more insurance agencies.
>
> "We're going to do business," I told Jack, and I've been a client ever since.
>
> When I walked him to his car after our first meeting, Jack asked, "Do you like boats?"
>
> "Nah, not really," I said. Then he showed me a picture of his boat.
>
> "Now I like boats!" I said. Jack invited me out for a cruise on the Chesapeake Bay, and that launched our enduring friendship.
>
> I've witnessed how kindly Jack treats people and never looks down on anyone.
>
> I've seen how he puts his family first. When we go out to dinner, most of our talk is about our children and grandchildren. He is a family man and loves his family with total devotion.
>
> —Phil Spector

We maintain close relationships with A-rated insurance underwriters as well, such as The Hartford, Travelers, and Chesapeake Employers—30 or 40 underwriters altogether. With those kinds of relationships, we can write almost any kind of insurance a customer needs.

Captive Gains

One of our major underwriters was the Insurance Company of North America (INA), and they named me as their agent representing the Baltimore area. I met with them at their home office in Philadelphia every other month, and became friends with the vice president of their commercial package business for the entire country, Michael Miles. Mike was probably the youngest vice president INA ever had.

One day in the mid-1980s, Mike came to see me at my office. "I want to talk to you about a business venture I'm planning. It's something that has never been done before."

I liked doing things that had never been done before. "Tell me more," I said.

Mike explained his idea to create a "captive agency." He was looking for ten agencies to invest $25,000 each as co-owners of a new underwriting company and agency, and send some of their business to it. It would be a separate corporate entity, so Diversified wouldn't have to sever any of its current relationships. Mike would leave INA to run the captive. "You're the first person I've asked to join," he told me.

The captive looked like a winner all around. I liked and trusted Mike. The captive would further diversify Diversified by giving us access to additional underwriting options and new market opportunities. My ownership gave me another asset with the potential for appreciation in value.

"Count me in," I said.

Mike brought on board the nine other agencies he needed and called the company Gail. For financial advantages, we incorporated Gail in Bermuda as a foreign captive, which "forced" us to hold our annual board meetings there—except when we held them in London.

Gail grew rapidly. Diversified's producers found plenty of well-suited prospects, including all of our car dealerships after the original underwriter went out of business. Other agencies copied our model and thousands of captives popped up around the country, but the trend worked to our advantage. Mike received attractive offers from agencies that wanted to buy Gail. After operating for about fifteen years, we sold Gail for a handsome return on our investment.

"THE MORE YOU GIVE, THE MORE YOU MAKE"

Everything Mike touched turned to gold, so when he approached me about investing in another company, I was all ears. He had his eye on a company in Virginia that wrote new-home warranties. The company was going bankrupt because warranty claims had spiked in the U.S., due in large part to poor-quality plywood imported from China.

Mike wanted to buy the company with the stipulation that the homebuilders purchased not only their warranty insurance through him but also their property and casualty insurance. He was looking for investment partners, and I didn't hesitate to write a check.

After five years, the company still wasn't profitable. "Be patient," Mike assured me. "We have to wait it out. This thing will turn around." And he was right. A few years later, it was making money and Mike received an offer to sell it at a large multiple of what we paid for it.

Settlement day finally arrived after eight months of negotiation with the buyers. But they backed out that morning. "We like your company, but we've found a better venture to invest in," they said.

"What are we going to do now?" I asked Mike.

"Well, we'll find another buyer," he said. "In the meantime, we'll continue to make a lot of money because we have almost every large residential home builder in the country in our program and they can't get their insurance anywhere else."

Mike was right again. A year later, we sold the company for double the amount of the offer that had fallen through.

"Jack, we were lucky with this one," he said. "But I'll tell you something I've experienced my entire life. The more you give, the more you make."

"Huh?"

"It's true."

"Interesting," I said. "What are you trying to tell me?"

Mike explained that he was donating a portion of his profit to Kids Smiles, a nonprofit dental clinic that provided free dental care to children in poor neighborhoods in Philadelphia. "They'd like to open a clinic in D.C. also," he said.

I gladly donated the seed money for the D.C. clinic, which treats about 3,000 kids every year. Kids Smiles invited me to the ribbon cutting and treated me like a hero, but Mike deserved all the credit.

Travel Perks

We wrote so much business with The Hartford that I became friends with the CEO, Ramani Ayer, and made their VIP list 25 times. As a VIP they invited me on an international trip every year! They called it "The Conclave," and the list of destinations would make Rick Steves envious—Hawaii, Vancouver, St. Petersburg, Dublin, Lisbon—fantastic places.

Dana went with me on most of them but one year, I took Lisa to Spain. Curiosity about Lisa and me got the best of the wife of another VIP. She cornered Lisa in the ladies' room. "I love your dress. You look so nice," she said.

"Thank you," Lisa said.

"I just have to ask you," she said, "is that your husband you're with?"

Not the first time I've been suspected of marrying a younger woman.

The Hartford spared no expense. Andrea Bocelli, who is recognized as the world's best-selling classical vocalist, gave me goosebumps when I heard him in Venice. On the trip to the French Riviera, the hotel concierge called on the day we were leaving. "Mr. Wurfl, would you like to take a limo to the airport, or can we take you by helicopter?"

"Helicopter, please," I said.

For entertainment on a trip to Vienna, the Vienna Boys' Choir sang and dancers performed for us. In the middle of the dance show, one of the professional couples came up to Dana and me and asked us to dance with them. They were going to teach us and the audience how to waltz.

In the average group of American tourists in Vienna, very few know how to waltz, so I surprised my professional partner. "My goodness," she said, "how can you dance like this coming from America? Where did you learn this?"

"Well, I'm originally from Vienna," I said. "I learned to waltz when I was five years old."

Since we were so close, Dana and I also took a side trip to my boyhood home in Gutenstein. I remembered the address and found the house where I lived for the first five years of my life.

In my mind, I could still picture the snails on the mountain trails. But were they real or a figment of my childhood imagination? We hiked the trails, and the snails were still there! But the restaurant owned by my father's friend where we had eaten lunch had been torn down.

PRAGUE ANGEL

We looked for the address my mother scribbled on the envelope of her letter to Tante Irma 62 years earlier

I took the letter that my mother wrote to Tante Irma with me in 2001 when The Hartford invited Dana and me on their VIP trip to Prague. My mother had scribbled her address on the envelope and I wanted to find her apartment.

Our hotel concierge couldn't read my mother's writing, but said, "I know someone familiar with that part of town who could probably figure out where it is." Sure enough, that person knew the street and gave us a map written in the Czech language.

Dana and I walked around Prague for 45 minutes trying to read the street signs and follow the map. All the buildings looked like dingy, Communist-era relics and gave us a chilly, eerie feeling.

Aha, there's her street!

But now where? There's no street number or apartment number on the envelope.

As we panned the houses, not knowing what exactly we were looking for, I spotted a gentleman across the street. "Maybe he knows something," I said to Dana. "It's worth a try."

The man had fair skin, radiant white hair, and icy blue eyes—striking, but a little unusual looking. I opened my mouth, and out came a question in German. I didn't even realize I was speaking to him in German. How surprised I was when he answered me in German!

"I lived on this street when I was a little boy," he told me. "Your mother's apartment is on this side of the street." He pointed. "There's the building. It's the middle unit."

I couldn't help thinking that he and my mother must have passed by each other many times between 1939 and 1941 while they both lived there. Dana snapped a few pictures of my mother's apartment and of me talking to the man. He stood with us for a few minutes, then said, "Much love and health to you," turned, and walked away. Dana snapped a few pictures of him as he left.

On our way back to the hotel we passed a Kodak store where Dana dropped off her roll of film to be developed. An hour later we picked up the envelope of pictures and flipped through them. *How wonderful to have these pictures of my mother's apartment! But what happened to the shots of me and the man who helped us find it?*

The only pictures of the man that turned out were the couple of him walking away from us. All the pictures of him standing with me were blank. *How unusual.*

On our flight home, Dana got curious about what my mother wrote to Tante Irma. "Dad, we have an eight-hour flight. Could you translate your mother's letter to me and I'll write it down in English?"

So I began reading and Dana began writing. I couldn't believe my eyes when I came to the end of the letter. This was the most unusual aspect of the whole experience with my mother's apartment in Prague.

"Dana, you're not going to believe how my mother closed the

Our Angel in Prague helped us find my mother's apartment

THE LOYALTY EFFECT

letter: 'To you with much love and health, I remain yours with many greetings for you and kisses for the boys. Gretel Wurfl.' "

Dana gasped, and we looked at each other. *To you with much love and health. Can that be right?* That's how the man who directed us to my mother's house said goodbye to us. I read it again. There was no mistake.

That man's glowing appearance—there was something spiritual about it. I had never believed in angels, but I had never experienced anything like this. Angels are people's helpers from God, right? If it weren't for that man I would not have found my mother's apartment. That's why Dana and I call him "our angel."

ALASKA RESCUE

The Hartford wasn't the only insurance company that nourished our relationship with adventures. In 1997, the CIGNA (formed when Connecticut General acquired the Insurance Company of North America) flew me and seven other "MVAs" (Most Valuable Agents) on the company jet to Alaska for a salmon-fishing expedition with the president of the company and other senior executives.

Over the course of a week, an outfitter's bush pilots flew us to various locations to fish. The rivers and lakes are surrounded by wildlands and rocks so the planes landed on the water or an island.

On the last day, we were fishing for red salmon in a remote lake almost 200 miles from civilization. The plane landed on a little floating island, then they took us to the fishing hole about two miles away in small aluminum motorboats. The water temperature was only 40 degrees tops so we bundled up in layers of clothes and bootfoot wader overalls to keep warm.

We were catching one red salmon after another but paused when we noticed a family of grizzly bears beside the lake—a mother and three cubs. Grizzly bears like salmon so we tossed a few over to them and they gobbled them right up. The mama bear must have figured, "They're feeding my babies so they can't be dangerous," and left us alone. But one of our guides stood by with his rifle at the ready just in case.

At the end of the day, we climb back into the motorboats to return to the island. The young kid handling the outboard motor guns the engine too hard

The grizzly cubs loved our salmon!

and the rear of the boat vaults into the air. The front of the boat, where six other passengers and I sit, dives underwater and spills us into the frigid lake.

Three of the passengers, including the president of CIGNA, yell that they don't know how to swim. But neither I nor anyone else can swim to the shore weighed down by soaking-wet gear and clothes.

The boat pops up from under the water, upside down. I help lift the president of CIGNA and the other non-swimmers onto the top of the boat. A gas can pops up next to me so I grab it to help stay afloat, and the others cling to the boat to keep above water. After ten minutes I feel my muscles lock up under the cold water from hypothermia.

Five more minutes pass and my muscles are barely moving at all. We hear our airplane approaching. Thank God the pilot sees us and makes an emergency landing on the lake. It takes everything in me to reach up and grab the rescue wire hanging from the plane, but I hold on and the co-pilot reels me in to safety. I rip off my waterlogged clothes.

The pilot pulls out a bottle of vodka and says, "Here, warm up!" and we pass it around. Nobody cares that he stashes liquor on his plane. The co-pilot radios ahead, and blankets are ready for us when we land at the outfitter's.

Everyone survived without harm. The only casualties were the cameras that were lost or ruined. Thankfully the professional photographer hired by CIGNA was in another boat so I have his striking highlights from the trip.

At the hotel, I stood in a hot shower for an hour. At dinner that night, the president of CIGNA swore everyone to secrecy about the accident. "If word of this gets out," he said, "I'll never be able to take agents fishing in Alaska again!"

Mentors

I couldn't have built Diversified into a Top 200 agency without the help of loyal mentors.

My first accountant, Gunther Boris, was one of the most astute, kind, and understanding people I've ever known. He worked for a large international accounting firm called Grant Thornton. Every time I needed advice about a financial decision or considered a major change in my operations I called Gunther and said, "I'd like your opinion about something." He'd talk it through with me over the phone or come to my office to meet. I'd usually include my good friend, attorney, and trusted advisor, Charles Yumkas, in those meetings.

As Gunther approached retirement, he introduced me to his younger colleague, Simpson Gardyn. "Jack, this young man, he's great," Gunther said. "He'll do all the day-to-day work for you, but I'll supervise it and always be there for you."

A few years later, Simpson left Grant Thornton to start his own accounting firm, a decision he credits me for, and Diversified signed on as his first client. Simpson became a lifelong friend and has handled my accounting for nearly 40 years. He always makes me feel like I'm the most important person in the world to him, and I haven't made any important decisions without consulting him first.

> ### It Gets Personal
>
> Financial matters are very personal, and when you work with someone's money you often progress from a business relationship into a friendship, and that's what happened with Jack and me.

And since both of our mothers were prisoners in Auschwitz, though mine survived, Jack and I grew even closer even faster.

Traveling together also helped develop our friendship. Jack, Phil Spector, Larry Cohen, and I began quarterly trips to Atlantic City. "Ritual" is a better word. We'd meet at 9 am, stop at 11:30 for lunch—always at the Woodstown Diner in New Jersey—and arrive in Atlantic City by 1 pm. We'd gamble for two hours, then buy peanuts and take a stroll on the boardwalk. We'd gamble a little more, eat dinner, and drive home.

Atlantic City was never about gambling—if Jack had $25 on the blackjack table he was so nervous you'd think he was risking his life savings—but always about camaraderie. Jack and I haven't been to Atlantic City in a while, but we still get together at least once a week for dinner.

—Simpson Gardyn, CPA

On Leadership

Since General Bob Ord became the fourth amigo on our fishing expeditions, I've counted him among my mentors. In every respect, Bob is one of the most wonderful human beings I've ever met. He's a West Point graduate and a former company commander in the jungles of Vietnam. As a three-star general, he led millions of U.S. troops throughout the entire Eastern Hemisphere. I do my best to emulate the way he leads, and the way he acts as a decent human being.

I've mentored countless new employees at Diversified and my main message is simple: "Insurance is the greatest business in the world. I'll teach you how we do things, and if you work hard and learn, you'll enjoy the work and make it your passion. Then there will be no limits on your success."

More to the Story

"It's been quite a ride"
By Phyllis Jeddry

I was only seventeen when Jack interviewed me for a job at Diversified. I sat at the round glass table in his office, and he asked about my work experience and why I thought I would be good for the assistant bookkeeper job. I told him about my business classes in high school, and that I loved accounting and was good with numbers.

He hired me before I left the office. I was so excited that I ran down the street to the bank where my mother worked and told her I found a job.

I wore a dress and high heels to work my first day and spent the entire eight hours on my feet filing documents. When I met my mother at the bus stop to ride home with her I said, "Mom, I can't stay at this job. My feet are killing me! I'm going to tell them I quit tomorrow."

My mother talked me into giving it more time, and over 40 years later, I'm still here.

Through my work in the accounting department, I learned how to read an insurance policy and was promoted to assistant account manager in the commercial lines department. I wanted to learn more about the insurance industry so I could grow in the field.

I tried first for the AAI, and passed. Then I passed the AU. I had doubts about my ability to make it through the ten college-level courses and exams for the highest designation in the field, the CPCU, especially when I had to take a break when my daughter was born. But Jack was like a second dad to me. "I know you can do it," he always told me. "I know you're smart because I see what you do for us."

Thanks to Jack's encouragement, I passed the CPCU, the biggest achievement of my professional career. He cares about his employees and appreciates everything everyone does at the company.

I worked my way up to a full-fledged account manager, and over four decades I've worn just about every hat in the office—except Jack's! Now I'm a vice president and the marketing manager, so it's been quite a ride.

ROCKETEERS
By Karen Wladkowski

Jack asked my sister, Phyllis, "Do you have somebody else like you at home who might be interested in being our receptionist?"

"I have a sister," Phyllis said, "but she only wears blue jeans."

Thanks, Sis, for that compelling recommendation.

But I jumped at the chance to go for an interview. I didn't wear blue jeans. I didn't have a driver's license so my father drove me and sat in on the interview. That was okay because I was afraid of Jack when I first met him.

Jack and my father chatted while I was out of the room taking the "Mental Alertness Test" that Diversified still gives all job candidates. When I returned, before he even looked at my test results, Jack offered me the job.

My fear of Jack quickly turned into admiration and respect as I discovered what a warm, fair, and generous person he is. Here and there I heard stories about his childhood. How could I not look up to somebody who had overcome so much adversity?

The more I got to know Jack, the more I wanted to stay at Diversified. He became a second father to me after I lost my dad. He offered advice, encouragement, and support whenever I needed it.

Jack gives people like me, with no experience, a chance, and encourages them to continue their education and move up in the company. Jack gave me the opportunity to get my insurance license and sell policies so I could earn commissions. I kept learning and growing, and now I have the title of vice president. I assist Jack with everything he does, though he jokes that now he works for me!

Around the office, people like me are called "Rocketeers" because they have nowhere to go but up, and hopefully they'll climb quickly.

Chapter 22

Returns

Lutherville, Maryland, USA
Colorado Springs, USA
Berlin and Dangast, Germany
Auschwitz, Poland
Various cities in Europe
Israel
1970-2012

I RECEIVED A call from a Jewish gentleman in England. "Are you Jochen Wurfl?" he asked.

"Yes."

"We've been looking for you in England for the past year because we have something to talk to you about. We thought you probably came here after the war so we advertised in all the British newspapers but didn't hear anything back. Now we think we've finally found you in the U.S."

"Yes, you found me," I said.

"I'm calling to tell you that we have recovered your grandfather's department store building in Bernburg, Germany, which the Nazis confiscated. We traced the ownership back to the Cohn family and have been searching for surviving family members. If you want to sell it, we have a buyer for you. The offer is $300,000."

"That's wonderful, thank you," I said. "I'll get back to you."

I couldn't accept any offers without due diligence. I found a large law firm in New York with offices also in Germany and asked their opinion. Their real estate experts in Germany appraised the building and told me that $300,000 was a fair price, so I told the English gentleman to go ahead with the sale.

Meanwhile, I had hired an attorney to look for the art that the Nazis stole from my grandfather. The lawyer found my grandfather's Lovis Corinth *Helle Rosen* (Bright Roses) painting at a museum in Braunschweig, Germany. The curator liked *Helle Rosen* so much that he hung it in the waiting room outside his office.

I worked on the search for the lost art with my cousin, Eric Cohn, who fled to Palestine after Hitler annexed Austria. We found what we considered iron clad proof of ownership. We showed the museum the

We recovered my grandfather's department store building in Germany

Helle Rosen
Photo credit: Wikimedia Commons

RETURNS

program from a Lovis Corinth art exhibit held in Berlin before the war. The exhibit producer asked my grandfather to lend *Helle Rosen* to the exhibit and listed his name in the program as the owner.

But Germans don't give things back easily. The curator denied the validity of the program listing and fought us for two years. My cousin Eric tried a different tactic—public pressure. He told our story to *Der Spiegel*, Germany's most popular magazine—on the level of *Time* and *Life* in the U.S.

Now the whole world would know that the German government refused to return a stolen painting to two Jews displaced by the Nazis. City officials were so embarrassed they agreed to give it back to us.

Eric wasn't interested in possessing *Helle Rosen*, so I considered buying out his share of the $350,000 sale price and hanging it in my house. But when I thought about how much the painting meant to the museum and Braunschweig, I offered to sell it back to them. Volkswagen, the largest employer in the city, put up the funds.

The good news is that a family treasure was recovered for its rightful owner, and I have a reproduction on my wall. The bad news is that my lawyers never found any of the other art the Nazis plundered from my grandparents.

But they did discover an irksome real-estate listing during their search. The buyer who paid us $300,000 for my grandfather's department-store building soon flipped it for $1 million.

"They cheated you," the art lawyer told me.

When I told my New York lawyer about it, he felt so bad that he offered, "I'll do anything you want and never charge you a cent." I liked him and didn't want to sue him, so I took him up on the offer. He recovered my grandfather's house and a few of his other properties, and we developed a friendly relationship over the years.

"You've come back to see me!"

In 1974, when Dana and Lisa were twelve and seven, I took them to Dangast to show them where I grew up and to meet Tante Irma's daughter, Waltraud.

During our stay, I asked Waltraud about Herr Pille, who would have been in his nineties. "If my teacher's alive, I want to visit him," I said. Waltraud told me that after he was released from the American prison a few years after the war ended, he settled in Varel, where she and Willy lived after they got married.

We drove to Varel and found him! He lived in a beautiful little apartment in a very nice section of town, and his two sons took good care of him.

Oh God, I can't describe what it felt like to see him.

He opened the door and recognized me right away. "My God! Jochen! Jochen!" Tears of joy streamed down his face. "You've come back to see me! And these are your children!"

We sat and talked for hours, and he remembered everything about Tante Irma and our school and our lives in Dangast. I thanked him for not turning in Peter and me to the Gestapo, and for giving me the best education of my life.

I kept in touch with Waltraud after our visit. Throughout the 1970s and 1980s, I invited her to Baltimore whenever she visited her mother and brother in Colorado. Waltraud wanted to go everywhere around Baltimore and also see the sights in D.C. and New York. I had so much to show her. Lisa liked Waltraud so much that she visited her in Dangast every summer while she was in college.

Still Searching For My Father

I was still missing pieces of the puzzle of what happened to my father during the war. In 2004, to look for more pieces, I flew to Berlin to visit Sachsenhausen, the first concentration camp where my father was imprisoned. Like many of the concentration camps, Sachsenhausen had been converted into a Holocaust memorial and museum.

"Do you have any records here of the prisoners?" I asked one of the archivists.

"Yes," she said. "Your timing is remarkable. We just received a shipment of records from Russia a month ago that had been stored in Moscow for the last 30 years."

The Russians were as interested in what happened at Sachsenhausen as I was because thousands of Russian prisoners of war died there. The archivist showed me the room where German doctors told the Russian prisoners to stand against the wall for their medical examinations and pointed to a hole in the wall. A Nazi soldier with a pistol stood on the other side of the wall and shot the prisoners through the hole.

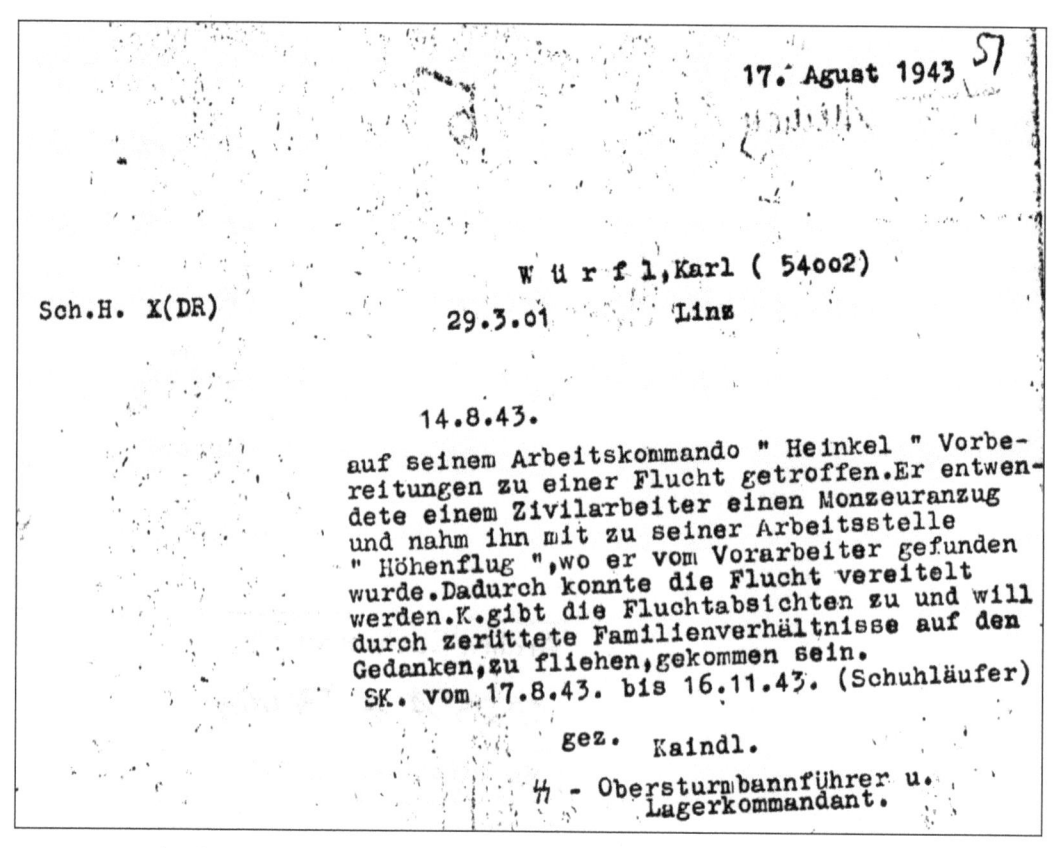

```
                                                17. Agust 1943  57

                           W ü r f l, Karl ( 54002)
Sch.H. X(DR)         29.3.01            Linz


              14.8.43.
         auf seinem Arbeitskommando " Heinkel " Vorbe-
         reitungen zu einer Flucht getroffen. Er entwen-
         dete einem Zivilarbeiter einen Monzeuranzug
         und nahm ihn mit zu seiner Arbeitsstelle
         " Höhenflug ",wo er vom Vorarbeiter gefunden
         wurde. Dadurch konnte die Flucht vereitelt
         werden. K.gibt die Fluchtabsichten zu und will
         durch zerüttete Familienverhältnisse auf den
         Gedanken,zu fliehen,gekommen sein.
         SK. vom 17.8.43. bis 16.11.43. (Schuhläufer)

                      gez.  Kaindl.
                      H - Obersturmbannführer u.
                             Lagerkommandant.
```

The documentation of my father's escape attempt from Sachsenhausen reports that, "K. admits the intention to flee and claims that the broken family situation gave him the idea of fleeing"

I gave the archivist my father's name and the dates of his imprisonment. "We'll look for his records," she said. "It will be a miracle if we find anything. Other people have come in looking for information and we didn't find anything for them, but we'll call you if something turns up on your father."

Three days later, she called me at my hotel. "We found him!"

The archivist found records of my father's escapes when he sneaked out to meet my mother, Peter, and me in Dangast. I walked the circle in the courtyard where I found out about his boot-walker punishment—they forced him to march in boots that squashed his feet and with rocks on his back until he dropped. She also found his transfer papers to the Mauthausen concentration camp near Linz, Austria, his hometown.

I felt both sadness and relief, and thanked the archivist for letting me have copies of my father's records.

MY TWO LIVES

FOND FAREWELLS

In the years approaching her 90th birthday, Tante Irma suffered from strokes, respiratory ailments, and cancer. In December 1982, she wrote to Waltraud that she wanted to see her once more and then "push off." When I visited Tante Irma in February 1983, it was a happy but difficult moment for both of us. We knew it would be the last time we saw each other, but neither of us said it out loud. In March, Waltraud called to tell me that Tante Irma had passed away.

Visiting Tante Irma and her son, Gernot, in Colorado Springs, circa 1980

I'll forever remember her incredible intellect, courage, and groundbreaking achievements. I'll treasure her fierce love for her own and her adopted children, and always be thankful that she infused in me the essential value of education and the love of nature.

I was moved by what her son, Gernot, said about her sacrifice for Peter, me, and Herr Pille: "For years my mother risked her life for these children. After the war, during war crimes trials, my mother testified on Herr Pille's behalf, and he was released. Few Americans realize that some Germans were human enough to not follow the Nazi Party's dictates about Jews." (Quoted in *Voices From The Other Side: Inspiring German WWII Memoirs*, by Jean Messinger.)

After Tante Irma's death, I wanted to keep in contact with Waltraud so I invited her, her son Jörg and his girlfriend Heike to go on vacation with me to Vienna. We had such a good time that the four of us vacationed every summer for ten years! We drove all over Europe—Prague, Paris, Munich—always to a major city.

On every trip, the four of us stopped by the docks on the North Sea and talked to Captain Blanke. We asked him, and later his son who took over for him, to take us fishing on the old boat I worked on as a boy. The days we caught eels and smoked them for dinner were the best!

Jörg and I became good friends and we still exchange emails at least twice a week. He and Heike broke up, but I still keep in touch with her as well. Waltraud's husband, Willy, was an artist and every year I'd bring home a couple of his paintings. His work is proudly on display not only at my house but also on Dana's and Lisa's walls.

Our vacations ended in the mid-1990s when cancer struck Waltraud. When I visited her at the hospital in Germany in 1998, we both knew she was close to the end, and she said goodbye to me. But a few days later, when I was back in Baltimore, she called.

Above, with Waltraud and Heike at the Dresden Zwinger Palace, 1993
Below, with Captain Blanke's son, Waltraud, and Heike admiring our catch on the North Sea, 1993

"Jack, would you do me a big favor?"

"Anything."

"Would you come and pick me up and take me to Baltimore? I would like to be with you."

"I will," I said, knowing that she would likely pass away before I could make all the arrangements. Those were our last words to each other. Two days later, at age 77, Waltraud died in Germany.

In Search of My Mother

I wish I could say that I had the same success in my quest for information about my mother at Auschwitz as I did with my father at Sachsenhausen. In 2006 I went to Auschwitz with my good friend and accountant, Simpson Gardyn, hoping for some kind of closure. Simpson's mother was also imprisoned there, and, thankfully, survived.

We hired a guide who was an expert in the plight of the Polish Jews. He showed us around Warsaw, including the Warsaw Ghetto where in 1943 about 13,000 Jews died in an uprising against their Nazi captors.

At Auschwitz, I searched everything in their files, even the train records, hoping I could find her name on a passenger list. They had absolutely no record of her. I had to face the fact that closure might never come.

After Auschwitz, Simpson and I spent

"Work Makes You Free" says the sign at the entrance of Auschwitz. Below: a crematorium oven.

RETURNS

several days in Israel. He had been there several times before, so between him and our tour guides, I received a college-level education in the religious and cultural roots of my mother and her family.

In all my travels, I find Israel one of the most fascinating countries in the world. It's the holiest place for the Jews, the holiest place for Christians, and the holiest place for Muslims. Sadly, I suppose that's why there hasn't been peace in Israel for thousands of years. When we visited the Jewish holy sites, they drove us in a bus with bulletproof windows and a Jewish soldier with a rifle next to the driver.

At the Wailing Wall with Rabbi David Katz (left) and Simpson (right)

It's also a beautiful country, with a desert, beautiful palm trees, and green agricultural areas. An amazing mixture. I returned to Israel six years later with Simpson and his rabbi, David Katz, for my "master's degree."

Chapter 23

LOVE AND PATIENCE

LUTHERVILLE, MARYLAND, USA, 2018

WHAT DOES IT take to stay married for 62 years? A lot of love and a lot of patience.

Zonia was one of the most beautiful women I had ever seen. We raised three lovely daughters, which in itself is amazing to me. It was wonderful just to be with Zonia. Loving each other was easy during the "for better" and "in health" times of our marriage. I needed to add more patience to my love when "in sickness" turned our times "for worse." Alzheimer's disease slowly debilitated Zonia for 30 years, and I watched the woman I married slip away.

Nohemy took care of Zonia for fifteen years, and Zonia loved Nohemy like another daughter. In the later years, I helped Nohemy lift Zonia into bed, but otherwise Nohemy bathed her, fed her, and did everything else she needed. If Nohemy needed extra help and I was away on business, she called her friends who came to help.

But the best care in the world doesn't stop Alzheimer's, and in the fall of 2018, the doctor told us that Zonia didn't have much time left. I'm grateful that at least she still recognized everyone.

On the morning of October 23, 2018, the nurse told us, "It's just a matter of hours now." The entire family—daughters, sons-in-law, and grandchildren—gathered in her bedroom. Zonia was breathing heavily and wasn't conscious or responsive, but we spent the day with her and said our final farewells.

Later that afternoon, the nurse suggested, "Why don't we let her die in peace? How about if you wait in the living room?" We moved into the living room, and within a half hour, the nurse came to see us.

"She has passed."

Chapter 24

NEXT GEN

LUTHERVILLE, MARYLAND, USA, 1996-2021

BY THE EARLY 1990s, Zonia and I were empty-nesters. By 2003 we were blessed with four grandchildren: Gabrielle Jaclyn Carroll, whom we call Elle, born in 1992; Thomas Robert Carroll, in 1995; Gillian Jade Roeca, in 1999; and Aidan Jack Roeca, born in 2003.

I'm so proud of all of them. I'm grateful that I hear from each of them because I understand that their jobs and schools and boyfriends and girlfriends are more important to their daily lives than their grandfather is nowadays.

Above: Thomas and Elle
Below: Aidan and Gillian

I want them to live their own lives—as I did. I subscribe to Kahlil Gibran's philosophy that parents are like a bow, and children are the arrow. Educate your children to make sure the arrow is perfectly straight because the day is going to come when you let go and shoot that arrow.

Elle is a lot like me. She loves to be with people all the time. After her year of teaching in Spain she came back and said, "That's what I want to do. I want to teach." She is currently studying for her Master of Arts Degree in Teaching, with a concentration in Early Childhood Education, at Towson University.

Thomas, he's brilliant and appreciates the value of education. He's already successful in the financial-brokerage industry in New York, has earned his Chartered Financial Analyst designation, and continues to work toward additional certifications.

Gillian was a biology and engineering major and a star field hockey player in college. She works as a biopharmaceutical consultant in Boston and is also quite an artist.

Aidan is another scholar-athlete. In high school, he got straight As while playing ice hockey, soccer, and football. He's now an engineering major at the University of Michigan.

With Lisa, Gillian, and Elle at my boyhood schoolhouse in Dangast

I took to heart the value of education that my parents and Tante Irma instilled in me. I've tried to instill that same value in my children and grandchildren. In 2012, I took Elle, Gillian, Dana, and Lisa to Dangast and showed them my two classrooms. I had told them the story of the school and Herr Pille, but it was more fun for them to see it.

Half of the building is now a museum for the North Sea estuary, explaining its eighteen-foot high tides and muddy *Schlick*. But the two classrooms have been preserved and look much the same as when I was a student. The same desks are still there. Lists of the names of former students and 30 or so of their pictures hang on the walls—including mine!

Elle and Gillian got the biggest kick out of seeing my picture. So did the museum docent. "My God, you're one of the old students!" he said, and told us that I was one of the few former students who ever came back to reminisce in the classrooms.

The same desks are still there!

Within days after the birth of each of my grandchildren, I opened a 529 college investment account for them. Between those funds and profits from my business, I was able to pay for half of their college educations.

That's great for my children and grandchildren, but I consider myself the main benefactor. They were blessed, but I was blessed beyond measure. I love that I could do it because I dearly love them, and I know they received an excellent education. That's the most important gift I could give them. And they were all such good students—I don't think that came from the Wurfl side of the family; they had to get it from Zonia's side.

NEXTGEN @DIVERSIFIED

I started Diversified with paper and pencils. Our technology in 1969 consisted of a few typewriters—one electric and the rest manual. We didn't even have a copy machine.

As soon as Dana joined Diversified full-time in 1984, I knew I would want her to own the agency at some point in the future. She worked with clients in account management, and she also led us into the computer age. We've probably spent over $2 million to upgrade from pencils to computers, but the return on investment is there in efficiency and an improved experience for our clients. Our automated systems make it possible to offer insurance from more than 50 different companies.

I offered my friend Tom Carroll a job at Diversified while he was in college because I thought he had what it took to manage the company someday. I had made that decision before introducing him to Dana. But Tom didn't accept my offer right away. He wanted to make sure he liked the insurance business apart from Dana and me so he took a job at another insurance company. A year later, he was ready to go all in with Diversified.

Because of the potential I saw in Tom, I tried something with him that I had never tried with anyone else I hired. I told him, "Tom, I'd like you to be my protégé. We'll put your desk in my office next to mine. You can listen to every phone conversation I have. Every time I meet a customer, go with me and sit in with us. Do the same thing I do for 40 hours a week, and in five years you'll know enough to run the company if anything happens to me."

Tom's apprenticeship was a blessing for both of us. He was a great guy to spend the day with, caught on to everything quickly, and had helpful suggestions for me. I was confident that he was the right man for my job—but not yet. I wanted a backup plan but was only in my fifties and still had a couple of decades left in my tank.

Tom Carroll, from golfing buddy to son-in-law to CEO

"Jack Poured Himself Into Me"

When I started at Diversified in April of 1986, I didn't know anything. When I wasn't listening in on Jack's phone calls or going with him to meetings, I read insurance books at a folding table in his office. He offered me open access and a great opportunity to learn and grow. I was ambitious, and Jack poured himself into me.

Jack introduced me to his clients and later handed over all of his prospects to me. He taught me everything about winning clients, and was never too busy to explain his ways to me or answer my questions.

But Jack never coddled me. He took me to see one client, Michael Arkin, who was also German. He and Jack were two peas in a pod. The first thing I noticed was that Michael had the same SCAN, laminate, fake pine conference table that we had in our conference room forever. I'm sure Jack asked Michael where he bought it.

Jack and Michael had the same accent and the same mindset about business. As I learned the business and became more competent, the two of them would sit next to each other, across from me, as I made a presentation. Then the two of them would tell me all the ways I could do better. It was truly learning under fire—some of it friendly.

The most important characteristic Jack modeled for me every day was his impeccable integrity. There cannot be a human being anywhere who can say that Jack did not keep his word. As a result, Diversified enjoys an incredible reputation with clients, insurance carrier partners, and team members. Jack taught me that if I make a commitment, I keep it.

Jack also has a gift for reading and connecting with people. He takes an interest in others. He values everyone he works with and never projects an air of superiority.

Even when he makes you keenly aware of how you didn't meet his expectations, he makes you feel good about it. At one meeting, a young man from one of our insurance carriers came in to review our agency production report, which shows how much business we did with them, the losses we had generated, and how much we were growing with them. Jack kept asking questions that the young guy couldn't answer. I felt bad for him, and I'm sure he was embarrassed.

But Jack folded the report and told him, "Look, I want you to do me a favor. Take this report back to your office, go through it with your boss, and when you understand it a little better, come back and explain it to me."

The guy told me later, "You know, Jack did me a great favor. He knew I was unprepared, but he didn't get mad at me, and he welcomed me back when I was ready."

That was Jack's way, and I did everything to be Jack. I used his language, his mannerisms. Everything. And, by the way, it worked pretty well.

—Tom Carroll
CEO and President

Under New Management

Just as I wanted a backup, I thought Tom should have a backup.

I met Sal DiPietro when he was a marketing representative for Fireman's Fund Insurance. He called on me to talk about what Fireman's Fund products could do for my clients. Due to Sal's persistence and their quality products, I did a lot of business with him.

At a meeting in 1986, Sal said to me, "A year ago I decided that my future should be on the agency side of the insurance business, not the company side. When you work for a company, you have a nice job and a nice salary, but there's always someone telling you what to do, and you can never own the business."

Oh, how I could relate to that!

Sal left Fireman's Fund and joined a small agency. A year later, he called me again.

"I should have talked to you about a job last year," he said. "The agency I joined made all kinds of promises they haven't kept."

I hired Sal, and for his first assignment, he helped integrate another small agency into Diversified. The owner, Jerry Cohen, had called me and said, "Jack, evidently I'm not as good as you are at running an agency because I'm not getting very far. I hear so much about you and I was wondering if I could become part of Diversified."

Jerry and I worked out a deal and shook hands on the acquisition. He and Sal knew and liked each other so it was a win-win, and Jerry stayed with Diversified for the rest of his career.

After onboarding Jerry and his staff, Sal worked side-by-side with Dana and Tom as a leader in the company. He came to me and asked if there might be any possibility of him buying an ownership stake in Diversified. I flashed back to when Keiser & Keiser denied me a share of their family business, so I allowed Sal to purchase a small tranche of stock.

I turned 83 years old in 2015, and I had no business running the company with so many talented younger people around. "You do it now," I told Tom, Dana, and Sal. I promoted Tom to President and CEO, and named Dana and Sal Executive Vice Presidents. I took the title of Chairman of the Board, and I meet with the rest of the board—Dana and Tom—every once in a while.

"Comfortably be like Tom"

As I developed my own clients and got busy with my book of business, Jack and I realized we had reached a crossroads. I would either continue on the path of building my individual client base, or take over the leadership of Diversified. Jack was ready to let go. "Tom, I want you to take over for me," he said, and named me the president of the company.

In my leadership journey, I first tried to be Jack. Then I tried to be *like* Jack. But I realized that I couldn't sustain either of those for the long term. Ultimately I learned how to look up to Jack but comfortably be like Tom.

If life is a ladder, Jack didn't even have a ladder when he started Diversified. He built the ladder. I picked up where he left off, and I am standing on his shoulders in terms of what we do.

Diversified will always maintain Jack's core values of integrity and care for others, and I've added my own modern flavor to them in our vision and mission statements. Our basic business model also remains the same. We will attract more clients, and keep the ones we already have. Pretty simple stuff that has worked for over 50 years.

Purpose-Driven Life

I believe that every person is on this earth with a purpose. One of the many reasons why Jack exists was to change the trajectory of a young kid who worked at Pine Ridge. There's not a single person on earth who did more to help me and give me the opportunity to manifest who I am than Jack.

My purpose is connected to Jack's. My responsibility is to be the steward of his legacy. When I show up to work every day, my primary obligation is to honor where we came from. Through Jack, God gave me this opportunity. As in the Bible's parable of the talents, I was given this gift to do something with it and to honor God in how I do it. Since I believe that living things grow, I will strive to make our future bigger than our past.

> I hope that when the story is told about my life, someone will say to me, "Tom, you got what you got, but you did well with what you got. You were a loving husband and father, an effective business leader, and you made an impact on others. Well done, good and faithful servant."
>
> —Tom Carroll
> CEO and President

Tom, Dana, and Sal have done an excellent job. I see things they do, and I think they're fabulous. I see other decisions they make and think I would never have done it that way. But that's a good thing. I don't want them stuck in the past, doing everything the same way I did it.

"You do it!" I told Tom, Dana, and Sal

Tom, Dana, and Sal work like a symphony together and make the big decisions jointly. They ask me what I think and if I agree, and I always say "Yes." They've carved out different roles and responsibilities for themselves, but you'll have to ask them exactly what those roles are because I have nothing to do with defining them.

> ### GROWING OR DYING
>
> Jack always recognized that Diversified had to be growing or we were dying. Around 1987 he called the first-ever Diversified planning summit.
>
> Jack, Tom, Bill Tracy, and I hunkered down for two days in a cottage at Caves Valley Golf Club.
>
> We worked through a SWOT (strengths, weaknesses, opportunities, threats) analysis of all we did well and how we needed to improve. One of the outcomes was the decision to hire more producers, aka sales agents. Tom led that charge, and we continued to grow the agency.
>
> One of the strengths we identified was Jack's commitment to forging strong personal relationships with the insurance companies we represent. Jack was peer-to-peer with the CEOs of the major insurance companies, such as Ramani Ayer at The Hartford and Hank Greenberg at AIG. Those CEO relationships translated into our producers getting appointments with top-level carriers and the best deals for our customers.
>
> Tom and I cherish our carrier relationships and always take the time to nurture them. That might mean a 45-minute phone call to make sure the company knows how important they are to us. Jack modeled that practice for us, and it will always be something that sets Diversified apart from other agencies.
>
> —Sal DiPietro
> Executive Vice President

CONCRETE VALUES

One of Tom, Dana, and Sal's big decisions was to move our offices out of Cross Keys in 2017. We needed more space but weren't happy with the way the national developer who bought Cross Keys let the property deteriorate. They chose a beautiful class-A building in Hunt Valley. I agreed with the move, though I miss my chopped-liver sandwiches from the Eddie's of Roland Park deli near the old office.

When we moved into the new offices, Tom gave every team member a concrete tablet with our company core values etched into it: Teamwork, Integrity, Positive Attitude, Pursuit of Excellence, and Servant Spirit.

Our company values are written in stone

"EATS AND BREATHES CORE VALUES"

I know what it's like to work in organizations that lack integrity, teamwork, and a servant spirit, so for me, Diversified's core values were the compelling reason for coming here. Diversified eats and breathes its core values, and that differentiates us from other companies.

In meetings, for example, everyone speaks up with their ideas but respects and adheres to the final decision. And if someone stops at another team member's desk and asks a question, that team member will stop what they're doing to help. Everyone defers their agendas to the goals of the team.

I take pride in weaving our values into conversations with new carrier partners, new customers, and prospective team members. They're in our heads, our words, and our actions, not just displayed on a mantel.

—Mike Papa
Director of Underwriting

Teamwork is people helping people when it doesn't help themselves. It happens at Diversified every day. Integrity shows when you mean what you say and say what you mean. It's what you do, not what you say you're going to do.

The Pursuit of Excellence involves lifelong learning, resilience, and making the most of every opportunity.

> ### THE FIGURE-IT-OUT GENE
>
> Our values make our workplace different from others. Integrity means we're honest and open with whomever we're dealing with.
>
> Watch team members interact on any given day and you'll see the teamwork. If you have a problem getting something done, a co-worker will step up to help. You don't have to ask, they'll just show up. Tom calls it the "figure-it-out gene," which is a combination of ingenuity, inventiveness, and creativity.
>
> You'll see service when someone is on the phone with a client and goes above and beyond to answer their requests. "Here are five insurance policy options for you, and here's the one that's the best coverage for the dollar." No one ever says, "Sorry, that's not my area." They'll search Google if they have to for answers to suggest.
>
> And our service extends to the greater community. Our in-house charity group, DII Does More, picks a charity to work with every year. We've collected and wrapped gifts for Santa Claus Anonymous. We've raised funds for other organizations through bull roasts, cook-off contests, making and selling calendars, and holding raffles and bingos. We've collected clothing, food, and household items to distribute to people who need them.
>
> DII Does More is another way that we live up to our company values and tagline: Build meaningful relationships, protect what's important, and serve when needed.
>
> —Sharon Stewart
> Senior Controller

A Positive Attitude is a boy in a horse stall that's piled to the top with manure. He's digging through it with his bare hands, happy as can be. "How can you be so happy in a pile of manure?" his friend asks. "Because there must be a pony in here somewhere!"

Team members with a Servant Spirit put the needs of their co-workers ahead of their own, even if they don't receive anything in return.

> ## "I FIT RIGHT IN"
>
> When I came to work here, I fit right in. It's like a family. I was in Odette's wedding, and team members came to my wedding.
>
> Jack hired me as a receptionist in 1991. In my performance reviews, he always gave me praise and told me how much he appreciated my hard work. It's nice to hear that you're valued. And Jack is like a father to me. He let me change my work hours so I could pick up my daughter from school and help her with her homework, and bring her into the office on snow days.
>
> The family atmosphere makes me look forward to coming to work every day. Who doesn't want to be around their family?
>
> Everyone at Diversified is encouraged to move up to new positions, and I moved into customer service on Tom Carroll's team. Tom trusts me to do an excellent job and never micromanages. I also see how Tom and all the producers build relationships with their clients. They go out to see them all the time so they know they can count on us. That's why Diversified has been around so long—I've handled many of the same accounts for 25 years!
>
> —Julee Hager
> Senior Customer Service Representative

Phyllis Jeddry says that the values have created a unique culture at Diversified. "It really is a family-oriented culture. Everyone cares about everybody. People not only want to do an excellent job, but they want everyone to work together. Regardless of our job descriptions, we all step in and help each other. You don't find that kind of understanding, compassion, and support in many other companies."

"THE ROOT OF THE TREE"

I started at Diversified in 2004 and was tasked with maintaining the unique company culture that Jack had established, and also refreshing it as times change.

Our culture originated with Jack's desire to trust people and develop relationships with them, both in business and personally. He believes that when we take care of our team members, they will take care of our clients. That's what Jack and Diversified are all about, and that's what we look for in the people we hire.

My mantra is: you can teach someone about insurance, but you can't teach them how to play well in the sandbox. Our job interviews include core value questions like, "Tell me about a time you went the extra mile for a customer," and "What have you done in your last job that makes you feel proud?" Jack also looks forward to sitting down and talking with new hires, and they like hearing his story.

I especially connected with Jack because my mother also came to America from Germany not knowing anyone and not speaking a stitch of English. Jack and I like to talk about German food. I've made him a few dishes, like goulash, and pick up smoked meats and German bread for him whenever I'm at Binkert's, a German market.

Jack is very kind. He wants team members to succeed in the

industry, and he's there to help them however he can. He wants to provide opportunities to create a career path the way he was given an opportunity. That might be through personal mentoring or DII University. Jack values education, and we established DII University in 2006 to make it convenient for team members to earn continuing education credits for insurance licenses and also to learn new skills, everything from Microsoft Office software to communication skills to yoga.

Jack lives his life by the motto, "Work hard, play hard," so it's not all just work around here. We try to have fun. "We sure do have good parties here," Jack always says. And we even have a Bocce Ball team!

Jack has always put people first, and that's why we have so many team members who have worked here for 10, 20, or 30 years or more. Jack is the root of the Diversified tree. All the additions we've made since are the branches. As I continue my career at Diversified, I will help the company continue to grow, following in his footsteps.

—Carin Hays
Vice President / Director of Human Resources

"The backbone of a business"

In 2021, with my 90th birthday a year away, it was time to relinquish ownership of the company. I gifted Dana a majority share of the stock, and Tom a minority share. Sal still had his portion. I'm so happy to leave the business in their hands because I'm confident they will always take good care of our customers and team members. My God, I'm so lucky to have them.

I'm excited about the future of Diversified. We have an all-star management team and staff, and the insurance industry is still the backbone of a business. Without insurance, you can't buy a car, a house, or a business. A business owner can't sleep at night without workers compensation insurance, liability insurance, and fire insurance.

And we are more diversified than when I started in 1969. With agents who specialize in a variety of insurance products and services, we offer the full spectrum, which increases sales and protects us from ups and downs in any one sector. We've added lines in areas I couldn't imagine in 1969, such as cyber liability, childcare, and home health care.

Innovation and change have been the keys to Diversified's success for over 50 years and will keep us relevant for the next 50.

Chapter 25

NINETY AND COUNTING

LUTHERVILLE, MARYLAND, USA, 2023

THE DAY BEFORE my 90th birthday, I walked through my office door and . . .

"Elle!" I screeched. "How is this possible? I thought you were teaching in Spain for two more weeks!"

"I changed my schedule to be home for your birthday!"

That was surprise number one.

Surprise number two was the deluge of birthday cards I received in the mail. And not just that day, but all week. Dozens of cards each day.

On my actual birthday, my phone started ringing at 6 am. I have relatives in so many time zones—from Big Odette in Florida to my brother Peter in Australia and all points in between—they woke me up, but their calls were wonderful gifts.

Since the COVID-19 pandemic hit in 2020, only ten or twelve team members came into the office on any given day. The rest worked from home. On my birthday, 50 came in to surprise me with a luncheon celebration—surprise number three. I hadn't seen some of them for two years so it was great to be together again. Karen ordered a deli tray from Eddie's of Roland Park that included my favorite—chopped liver.

Two nights later, Dana invited me over for dinner.

I walked in her front door and . . .

I dropped my keys on the floor. "Thomas! You came home from New York!"

"I wanted to be here for your Father's Day brunch on Sunday!"

That was surprise number four. Dana said she was worried that all these surprises would give me a heart attack. But she kept going with more.

On Sunday, which is Father's Day, Dana and Tom pick me up and take me to the Baltimore Country Club for my Father's Day brunch. "Elle and Thomas are meeting us there," they tell me.

BCC is a gorgeous club, and the weather is perfect. As we walk to our table, I stop to admire the flowers around the patio and the view of the trees and rolling hills along Roland Avenue. I can see Cross Keys from there.

"Come on, Dad," Dana calls.

We walk a little farther, and I hear clapping. *What happened? Why are the club members clapping?*

Then I see Elle and Thomas. And Lisa, and Nohemy, and Simpson, Larry, Mark, Phil, and so many more faces. *Oh my gosh, all these people are here for me!*

I look down at a cake. "That's my shrimp boat from Dangast on the cake! How did you do that? It's so beautiful. We can't eat it."

The three-hour brunch flies by. The food looks delicious but I hardly eat anything because I'm so happy to talk to everybody—25 people who mean so much to me.

To top it all off, Tom and I played six holes on the golf course.

"The best birthday of my life!"

It was the best birthday of my life. It's all I talked about for days afterward, maybe weeks.

Better than my 80th birthday, when I water-skied on the backs of dolphins in the Cayman Islands. It was the best even though I have a couple of medical issues—atrial fibrillation, and my colon was removed in 2021 after cancer returned. They make me uncomfortable at times, but nothing is life-endangering at the moment.

It was my best birthday because I appreciate talking to the people close to me more than I ever have. With fewer responsibilities, I've become a better listener. I used to do all the talking and tell everybody what to do. Now I listen to what they have to say, sit back, and enjoy watching what they do and how things work out.

I can enjoy life despite my physical limitations. My fishing buddies tell me, "Jack, we hope we feel as good as you do when we're 90."

Nohemy is a big reason why I feel so well. After Zonia died, I asked Nohemy to stay with me. She was part of the family, and I expected I would need her help someday. I was right. She's been my angel for twenty years now. She shops, cleans, and drives me to appointments. She also helps me keep Zonia's memory alive. Not a day goes by without Nohemy talking about her.

When it's not my birthday, my office is my happiest place these days. I go in to review the company's financial statements and manage my retirement accounts. That's the kind of mental challenge I need to stay sharp. The worst thing for me to do is sit at home and do nothing. That would take more years off my life than heart disease or cancer!

Musings of an Insurance Man

Anne Frank said of her diary, "It seems to me that later on neither I nor anyone else will be interested in the musings of a thirteen-year-old schoolgirl." She could not have been more wrong. I hope that, later on, readers are also interested in these musings of a 90-year-old insurance man.

As I look back, I wish the suffering that my family and I, Anne Frank, and millions of others endured during my first life had never happened. It was unfathomable; not even human. But it's good for people to realize the kinds of atrocities human beings are capable of inflicting on one another so we make sure they never happen again.

In my second life, I've had many golden years. I tell everyone, "Have a passion for the work you do. Enjoy it." Work should be a pleasure. And don't just work. Play. "Well, what about money?" some ask. I tell them I never thought about making a lot of money. All I wanted was enough to take care of my family. My advice is to focus on your passion, and the money will come.

May children who grow up in wonderful situations cherish their freedom and understand that life isn't as easy for everyone. May those who grow up in difficult circumstances take heart in my living proof that they can find freedom and overcome obstacles. I hope my story gives every reader the confidence that whatever they want to do in life, it can be done.

Happy Birthday, Jochen!
By Dana Carroll

Sharon Stewart, our Controller, who has been with Diversified since 1981, told me that for her father's 90th birthday, she asked 90 people to send him a birthday card. "That's a great idea," I said. "We can do that for Jack."

Karen, Jack's assistant, contacted family, friends, current and former co-workers, customers, and colleagues—people that my father meant a lot to—and let them know that his 90th birthday was coming up.

We were overwhelmed by the response, especially my father. Not only by the number of cards—110—but also by the memories they evoked and sentiments about my father's impact on their lives.

"There were so many beautiful cards," my father said, "and so many beautiful things people wrote. But I'm really not as wonderful as they say I am."

Jack's 90th birthday cake. The image is Willy Hinck's painting of the shrimp boat that Jack worked on as a boy in Dangast

I love THE DAD YOU ARE.

6-15-2022

You give no-matter-what,
to-the-ends-of-the-earth love.
Your selfless caring says a lot
about the kind of man you are—
a man I'm grateful to call my dad.

HAPPY BIRTHDAY

Happy Birthday To You Dad. You Are So Special To Me, + I Am Thankful Each + Every Day For You. We Are Always There For Each Other, Yesterday, Today + Tomorrow.
Love You Dad + Happy 90TH B Day
Dan

NINETY AND COUNTING

> There are only two ways to live your life. One is as though nothing is a miracle. The other is as though everything is.
> — Albert Einstein

Jack —

You could easily say that your life is a miracle. But that would sell short your own creative hand that has built an incredible journey. I have been so fortunate to be a witness and a part of that story. Your life and all that you created is a blessing to so many people. Your family, your friends, your associates, clients, advisors, employees — and one incredibly fortunate son-in-law. You have shared so much with me and I am incredibly grateful for all of it. Happy Birthday — we celebrate you and give thanks for having us along for the ride!

With love + admiration,

Tom

BIRTHDAY! HAPPY

Dear Mr. Jack
Happy birthday.

I am so happy to be with you on this especial day.
There is no one else like you. You have gifts that only you can give to people around you. You have blessings others can only receive through you.

I know God designed every detail of who you are.
I hope you and I will be togather for many more years.
Feliz cumpleaños mi amigo te quiero mucho.
God bless you always.

Love Nohemy

Dear Jack,

YOU'RE THE KIND OF MAN
MORE MEN SHOULD BE LIKE—
GOOD TO YOUR FAMILY AND FRIENDS,
GENEROUS AND THOUGHTFUL,
TRUE TO YOUR WORD.

THAT'S WHAT MAKES
CELEBRATING YOU SO EASY.
THAT'S WHY THIS WISHES YOU
ALL THE HAPPINESS YOU DESERVE,
WHICH IS PRETTY MUCH
ALL THE HAPPINESS IN THE WORLD.

Happy Birthday to you! This card was so easy to pick out. So True. I can't tell you enough how much I appreciate the opportunity you have given me.

Most importantly, it has been such a privelege to have you as a friend, role model and mentor. Have a great Day!

Sal

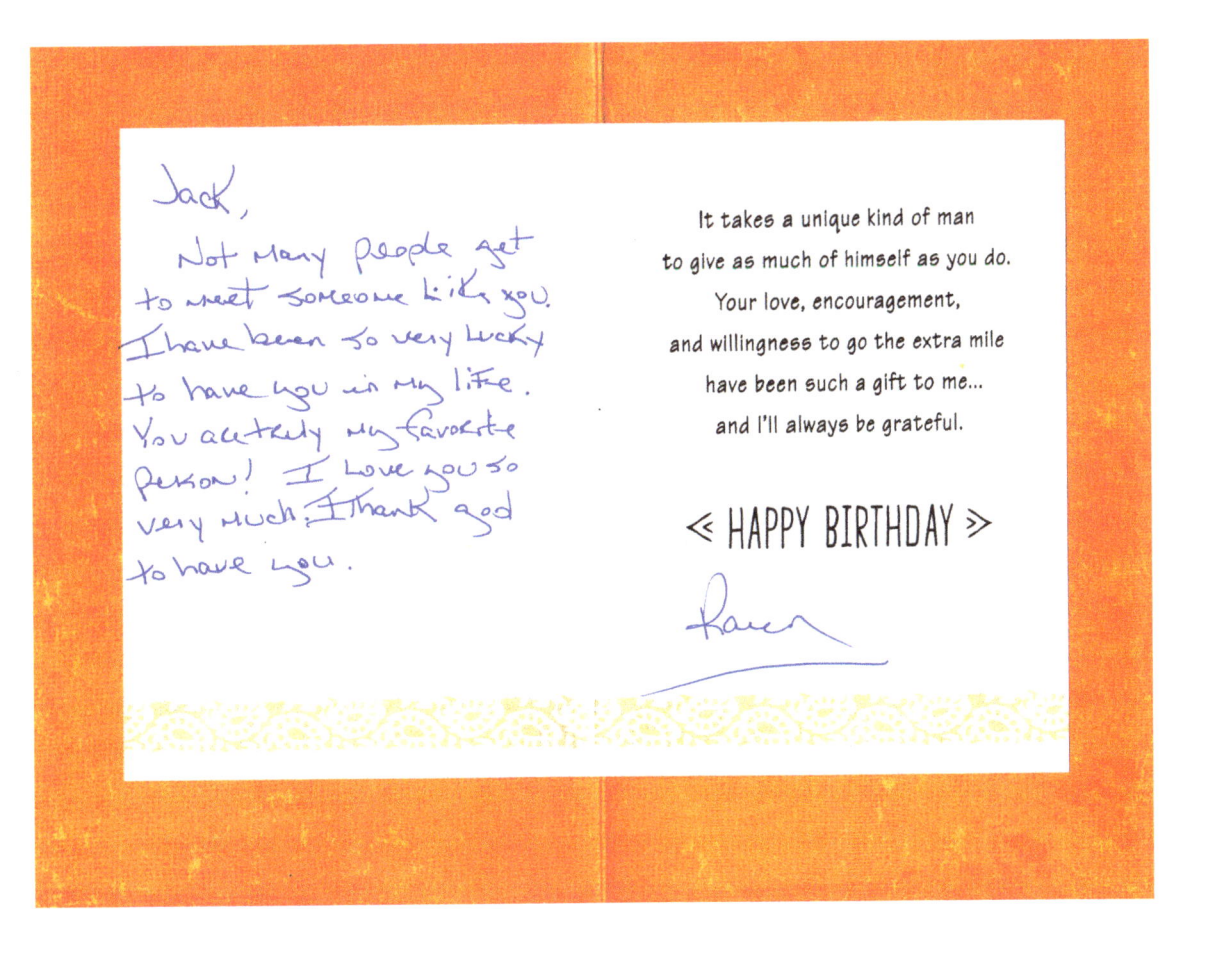

Jack,
   Not many people get to meet someone like you. I have been so very lucky to have you in my life. You actually my favorite person! I love you so very much. I thank god to have you.

It takes a unique kind of man
to give as much of himself as you do.
Your love, encouragement,
and willingness to go the extra mile
have been such a gift to me...
and I'll always be grateful.

≪ HAPPY BIRTHDAY ≫

Karen

Dear Jack

I can honestly say my life changed the day I met you. Over the years I have learnt so much from your wisdom. The way you conduct yourself in business with such honesty & integrity. The caring you show in dealing with people whether its with your employees business associates or just friends. I have taken these lessons and tried to incorporate them in the way I conduct my life. And than again as I always remind you I thank you for the modest success I have accomplished in business. I owe it all to you. When over 35 years ago you encouraged me to venture out on my own and differed would be my first client. I can never thank you enough for all you have done for me. May you have

The greatest 90th year of your life, is with good health and happiness, and my G-D grant you many more years of good health and happiness. May we continue to have our weekly dinner

Your best friend

Simpan & Debbie

Happy Birthday

June 2022

Jack —

Guys who face challenges with courage,
and always take care of what matters most.

Guys who give their best each day
and prove anything is possible.

Here's to the good guys —
like you.

With so few words, this card speaks volumes about the amazing human that you are! I feel very honored & blessed to have been able to be a part of your world... even if just a few short years. You have definitely set the bar high for the rest of us, but I will continue to strive for it!

HAPPY BIRTHDAY

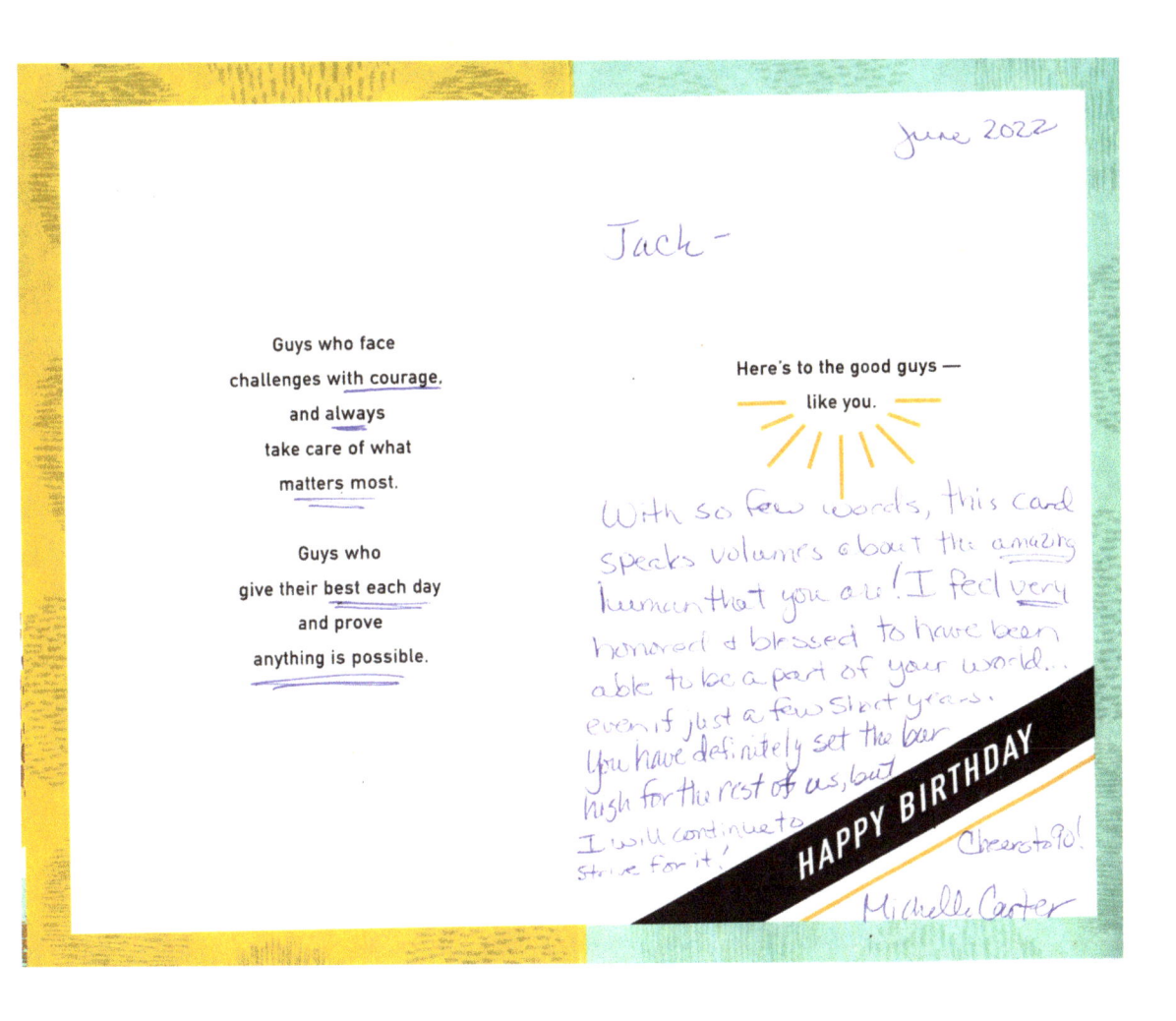

Cheers to 90!

Michelle Carter

P.S.
One of my favorite memories was our trip to the Caymans and you flying across the water on the fins of dolphins! I believe you were celebrating 80 that week. !:)

Dear Jack,

Happy Birthday to one of the most inspiring people I have ever met!

I chose this Secretariat birthday card for your 90th Birthday for 2 reasons. First of all, because you and I both love Secretariat and this was one of his most thrilling wins at the Belmont Stakes and Triple Crown, 1973!

Secondly, because in many ways, you remind me of Secretariat. The story of Big Red was more than a story about a great racehorse. It's a story about the heart, determination and courage that empowered Secretariat and all the people around him to achieve remarkable goals. That's you Jack – and I salute on your special day and special year.

It has been a privilege to capture your story through our interviews and I look forward to hearing about all your remaining chapters. Many blessings to you!

Your friend,

Diane Lonsdale